Stark Raving Mad

Musings of a Classical Liberal Economist:

2007-2009

JOIN, or DIE.

Terry Easton

NextGen Publishing Company
www.nextgenpub.net

First Edition published September, 2009.

Photography , cover and design by Erica Simone (www.ericasimone.com) and set in Minion Pro and Bell Gothic Std types.
Printed and bound in the United States of America and the United Kingdom.

Library of Congress Cataloging-in-Publication Data is on file with the Library of Congress. Library of Congress Control Number: 2009939754

Easton, Terry

Stark Raving Mad, Musings of a Classical Liberal Economist: 2007-2009 by Terry Easton
-1st ed.
p. cm.
Includes index.
ISBN-13: 978-0-9749694-3-5 (paperback: alk. paper)
ISBN-10: 0-9749694-3-5 (paperback: alk. paper)

1. Title [1. Economics - Essays. 2. Political Science - Essays]

FIRST PRINTING

NextGen Publishing Company
Burlingame, CA 94010
http://www.nextgenpub.net

CONTENTS

Part I - Columns & Commentary

CONTENTS

Part II - The American Economic System

Introduction

Over the past two years, I've had the pleasure of writing a series of columns for Human Events on the subject of economics - and how it affects our lives in the real world.

I have also been a teacher of high technology, management and economics at several universities spanning a 30-year carrier.

But, perhaps most importantly, I have been an entrepreneur and businessman who has had to meet a payroll of several hundred people, and it is the day-to-day living in the real world that provides the best experience for understanding the timeless truths that economics teaches, starting with the old truism: "there's no such thing as a free lunch!"

The term economics comes from the Ancient Greek word οἰκονομία (oikonomia, "the management of a household; it's administration"). Oikonomia is created from οἶκος (oikos, "house") and νόμος (nomos, "law" or "custom"), hence, Economics originally was simply the "rules of the house(hold)". The household has grown to include the world.

Until the turn of the 20th Century, Economics was commonly known as "Political Economy", and was taught as such in the institutions of higher learning on both sides of the Atlantic. Free-market philosophers such as Adam Smith & David Ricardo sought to understand and rationalize the broader concept of economics as applied by the state in the form of the king. The goal of forward-thinking Economists was to conceptually develop the "ideal market" based on natural law as passed down from God, and the free will of man, rather than the personal whims of an all-powerful ruler.

Then Karl Marx wrote his (in)famous Das Kapital, which provided the (false) economic justification for totalitarian fascist and communist dictators, their new "bible". So-called Progressivism which emerged in the early 1900's and continued through FDR's rule, sought to soften the strong fist of totalitarianism while expanding an ever stronger, more powerful big government-big business partnership. And the moral destruction continued.

Although Dwight Eisenhower warned Americans about the caustic collusion between powerful politicians and giant special-interest businesses operating under the name "the military-industrial complex", Washington, D.C. continued to expand its reach and control over all aspects of society. New agencies have appeared to regulate every aspect of one's life: the EPA, the Department of Commerce, the Department of Education. What kind of toilet bowl you can buy to what light bulbs you may use are now directed by government "Czars". In FDR's Administration there was more honesty. They simply called them "Dictators".

The founding fathers had designed the Constitution, chocked full of checks-and-balances and a Bill of Rights, to protect the people from an over-powerful government. They had designed a bottom-up system of government, the United States of America. Each sovereign state was responsible to its own citizens. Senators were appointed by each of their own state legislatures. "It's a Republic, Ma'am, if you can keep it!", uttered by a jubilant Benjamin Franklin at birth of the Constitution in Philadelphia, would still have been recognized even as recently as the 1950's.

This book is a collection of musings about what is happening in our world in the early days of the 21st Century.

As an Austrian Economist, I believe in the rational individual and the free market of open choice between the consumer and the supplier. I am against price-fixing, monopoly protection, government subsidy, and the myriad laws designed to take from the guileless consumer and give to the corrupt crony of a corrupt politician. I am in favor of honest money fixed to a gold standard that can't be counterfeited by the flick of an official government printing press switch. I am against the wacky - but popular in the seats of power - notion that a country of 305 million complicated, thinking, independent citizens can be managed by a few "clever" bureaucrats from a centralized location. It didn't work in the USSR, and it will eventually fail in the USA.

Perhaps the irony of ironies is that Vladimir Putin, a former KGB officer and head of modern Russia, warned the US against going down the disastrous path of progressive socialism at the 2009 annual meeting of the worlds mighty and powerful in Davos,

Switzerland. "Been there, done that" is what he essentially said. Will we listen in time?

Today, the USA has morphed into United "State" of America.

It's as if - as Glenn Beck, that 21st. Century Paul Revere has said - we are trapped in the Matrix where we are all asleep in some drug-induced coma while the software - the Program - is secretly running beyond our awareness. And the goal of the Program is control, total control over all aspects of our money and our lives.

It's not about Democrats versus Republicans. Both parties have deteriorated into caricatures of their former selves. John Kennedy would as likely be shocked at the Democrats in power today as Dwight Eisenhower would be flummoxed by the Republicans. Twiddle Dee-Twiddle Dum politics means that "throw the bums out" simply replaces the politicians with another set of bums - to be tossed out once again. The system has stabilized, through gerrymandering the voting districts and big-lobby money, into a two-party razor-tipped pendulum swinging back and forth. Meanwhile, it's rope is winching ever lower like the Pit and the Pendulum, creeping ever closer to destroy the ultimate freedom of the trapped "Freeman".

Part I presents my columns from Human Events (www.HumanEvents.com) which have been kindly run by Editor extraordinaire Jed Babbin.

Human Events, founded in 1944 in Washington, D.C. is the nation's oldest conservative newspaper, with both a weekly printed edition and a daily Internet-based edition. It is owned by Eagle Publishing, Tom Phillips' attempt to undo some of the wacky things happening inside the beltway today.

Along with Human Event's sister publishing enterprise, Regnery Books, and several excellent financial newsletters written by long-time friends such as Mark Skousen, Tom's outreach to the "classical liberal" seems to be doing a pretty good job.

Part II is a work-in-progress, an essay in chapter form, of the philosophy of the American Economic System.

But it is more than that.

A just economic system must first be a moral economic system, and thus the exploration of what makes a system so, be it a government, or another collection of people, needs to be explored. For my Econ 1A Macro Economic students, coming fresh out of a government-run high school, this sometimes seems like heady, even revolutionary stuff. For the person who has been fortunate to have heard the Beetles live the first time around, well it may seem like just plain common sense.

Here is a friendly challenge: take the 2 minute interactive test on freedom at: www.theadvocates.org and see how you score. Then after reading the book, take the test again. You may be surprised.

A big thank-you needs to go to Dr. Art Robinson, resident genius of the Oregon Institute of Science and Medicine and publisher of Access to Energy, the delightful newsletter written for the regular reader (www.OISM.org). With every delicious issue, Art runs his famous "Stark Raving Mad" commentaries on yet another government boondoggle or bureaucratic nightmare. He could write a book every fortnight on this subject alone!

One final thank you is due to my long-suffering friend, companion, intellectual sparing partner and wife of nearly 40 years, Susan Easton. Susan's new book, Notes From a New Europe is her reporter's collection of Human Events articles also appearing over the past several years. Susan writes about the European world through the eyes of a journalist and theologian, with a bit of humor thrown in. She usually writes about politics, a field in which, as a theologian she observes, "forgiveness is much needed." I should know.

Terry Easton
London, England
September, 2009

SECTION I

Musings of a Classical Liberal

JOIN, or DIE.

$3.50 Gas & 13,500 DOW: What's Going On Here?

JOIN, or DIE.

When I get together with my economist friends, I'm told we're now in the boom times. Inflation is under 3%, and the US economy is "the gift that keeps on giving!"

Unemployment is at a 4.5% record low and the stock market is approaching 14,000. We seem to be living in a "Goldilocks economy," with everything just right.

But then my normal friends ask me why gasoline is headed for $3.50 a gallon -- and how can gasoline keep going up without killing off the stock market's golden goose? After all, the housing market is already melting down. Last year when oil shot up, the DJIA tanked.

What's going on?

The free market is a straight-forward process. A willing buyer gets together with a willing seller to trade goods or services.

As long as no one tampers with the marketplace, everything works pretty much as it should. But it's often hard for folks to resist making things "just a little bit better". And then the government steps in to lend a helping hand...

First, the bad news: the free market isn't really as free in the US as we like to think. Especially when it comes to oil.

There's a whole bunch of government intervention at work. Our economy is more like a "mixed economy" -- it's partly free and partly highly regulated and government owned and controlled.

Left to its own, competition would naturally drive the price of gas rapidly downward -- back to a buck a gallon that it sold for in the late 90's. Maybe lower.

But whenever a legislature passes laws to manipulate a market (remember, they call it "helping"), they almost always come down on the side of the producers and against the consumers. Energy is the best example of this natural law at work.

There are 5 main reasons why gasoline seems so expensive –and may be headed down the road in California to $5 per gallon in the short run.

The cost of gasoline is the sum of these 5 items: crude oil cost, refinery costs, dealer & transport costs, taxes, and profit margin. Public policy permeates all aspects of this equation.

When either the supply is cut or held back artificially or the demand increases, the price shoots up. Sometimes, like today, both can happen simultaneously.

Take crude oil costs.

In 1999 a barrel of the benchmark Brent Crude Oil (LO, IPE) cost $10 to buy. Today, it sells for around $65.

The vast majority of the world's oil is owned by OPEC -- a producer cartel that would be illegal to operate in the United States. It consists of the giant government-owned oil companies of Saudi Arabia, Iran, Venezuela, Nigeria, Libya, etc., many of which are politically unstable -- and unfriendly to the U.S.

OPEC is a supra-government-level price fixing system which sets output quotas to keep up the profits of the producers. Tiny producers like Exxon, Shell, BP & Total follow the prices set by the "big boys."

When demand is high, OPEC has pricing leverage over the marketplace. At a so-called "sunk" cost of $5 per barrel to pump the crude oil out of the ground, Saudi Arabia stands to make $60 per barrel profit. OPEC can hold back lots of oil from the market-place and still make a profit for its governments.

In the USA, on the other hand, most cheap oil has already been extracted. It now costs over $25 per barrel -- and is rising monthly.

The ability to tap most old and new oil fields inside the U.S. has been made illegal, and new "made in America" supplies have been forcefully held back. This has mostly been legislated in the reasonable public policy of a green ecology -- and helped along by the kindly old oil companies, struggling to rebuild their depleted treasuries drained by the bad old days of $10 per barrel oil.

The bottom line: overall crude oil supply is presently limited -- by fiat.

Overseas demand is soaring too, fueled by the millions of Chinese drivers who now have bucketfuls of dollars - which we eagerly ship them daily -- to buy their own new cars.
Add in a few regional wars, oil field terrorist incidents and assorted natural disasters, and the overall global supply-demand balance has tipped toward a shortage of ready supply. Up shoot the gas prices.

Add just 10% more domestic oil to the equation and the price of oil would likely crash below $20 per barrel.

A barrel of oil holds 42 gallons. This can be converted at the refinery into about 44 gallons of gasoline and other fuels & lubricants (so-called processing gains results from adding other chemicals to the mix). In theory, then, a gallon of crude oil is to-day worth roughly $1.55, or less, on the world's markets.

Next, add in refinery costs.

Refinery costs (including delivery to the refinery by pipe-lines or ships) push the price up to about $2.25 per gallon of un-leaded gas (RBOB, NYMEX.)

This is an increase of 67%. Surely there's a way to cut these costs?

Although gasoline usage has increased over 25% since 1975, there have been no new refineries built in the United States for over 30 years. The last refinery was started up in Garyville, Louisiana in 1976. US refineries are old, inefficient, and prone to breakdowns and frequent maintenance. And the blockbuster refineries are located in the energy-friendly but hurricane-prone states of Texas and Louisiana. They are running at maximum output.

The result? Many are off-line at any moment (lowering the production supply of gasoline). And we are now forced to import both crude oil and unleaded gasoline from outside the US. Domestic refineries are down to 89.5% utilization. We're still recovering from fires and hurricanes that happened back in 2005 and 2006.

The solution is simple. Build more refineries. Right?

Wrong.

Both state and federal government laws, the dozens of environmental agencies, and green-movement lobbies coupled with a good dose of NIMBYism have effectively killed off the construction of modern oil refineries inside the United States for the past 3 decades. Demand goes up but domestic supply can't easily be increased -- especially when demand peaks over the summer driving season starting this Memorial Day.

In addition, there isn't a single US gasoline. There are literally hundreds of "mixes," most mandated by law. Government edicts have forced additives like MTBE (which destroys the drinking water supplies) and less powerful but more expensive ethanol (which causes breathing problems) to be mixed into each modern gallon of gasoline. And each state can be different.

The result? Less real gasoline per gallon means less energy-per-gallon to power your car engine, and lower miles-per-gallon result. You have to use more gas to go the same distance. Which means the overall demand for our weakened gas goes up even more.

California is the worst culprit. The state has forced its in-state refineries to concoct a unique and expensive mix of gasoline sold nowhere else in the world. No more state refineries can be built.

As the California Energy Commission itself points out: "In fact, from 1985 to 1995, 10 California refineries closed, resulting in a 20 percent reduction in refining capacity. Further refinery closures are expected for small refineries with capacities of less than 50,000 barrels per day. The cost of complying with environmental regulations and low product prices will continue to make it difficult to continue operating older, less efficient refineries."

And only a few refineries outside California are willing to expensively modify their non-California gasoline and ship it into California in any meaningful way.

The effect is obvious. Gasoline which sells for $3 a gallon in Washington, D.C. sells for $4 a gallon in San Francisco.

May 23, 2007

The Wacky World of Oil: Why Gasoline Will Hit $4.00 a Gallon this Summer

JOIN, or DIE.

The price of gasoline is the sum of 5 items: crude oil cost, refinery costs, dealer & transport costs, taxes, and profit margin.

Artificial shortages in crude oil and refinery capacity coupled with soaring demand for gasoline in China and India and the rest of the developing world have created a tight supply situation with very little reserve "cushion."

Under these conditions, the phenomena of marginal pricing and supply kicks in. A tiny decrease in supply, perhaps a fraction of 1%, can cause the selling price to shoot up by 5 to 10% or more. Likewise, a slight increase in supply can quickly deflate the gasoline price balloon.

Dealer and Transport costs inside the United States directly contribute to the overall high price of gasoline.

In a competitive market, dealer and transport costs (pipelines & trucks) adds under 9% to the overall costs. This includes the station's overheads & profits, along with payroll and property taxes.

Throughout the USA, the number of gasoline stations has been systematically cut in half since the 80's. This cuts supply outlets and reduces retail outlet competition.

In California and elsewhere, states now require gasoline stations over a certain age to dig up and replace their worn out underground storage tanks and clean up these alleged "hazard pollution site" -- whether they are leaking or not. Independent, privately-owned gasoline stations can't afford the hundreds of thousands of dollars to comply, so they often close down.

The big chains -- owned by the oil companies and refiners -- wind up with an ever-growing market share of the local retail market. The business becomes vertically-integrated due to well-intentioned government mandates. This makes it easier for the market producers to set prices up and down the supply chain to the advantage of the supplier and the disadvantage of the consumer.

The result: gas prices go up.

Fortunately, car manufacturers are making both lighter and smarter cars which burn gasoline much more efficiently then they did in, say, 1974. Cars got 14.2 miles per gallon back then. They now get, on average, 27.5 mpg (not counting so-called light trucks, which lots of people still buy in the guise of SUVs).

So consumption for gasoline, per automobile, has actually been falling.

But when gas was way below $1 a gallon, Americans fell in love with SUV's. And why not? They are safer, more flexible and can carry more stuff and kids. Every soccer mom knows this. This love-affair is still going on today. So for many suburban middle-class families with kids, the great gas squeeze is beginning to be felt.

But taxes -- at every level -- are the major component of gasoline.

All states tack on the standard Federal Excise Tax and a State Excise Tax, and many cities and counties throughout the USA add local sales, usage and consumption taxes. New York, California and a dozen other states add a sales tax to top it off.

That's right, they tax the tax.

Add in the taxes on the oil drillers, the oil producers, the oil distributors, the oil refineries, the shipping companies, the trucking companies, the pipeline companies and the local gasoline stations, and perhaps 50% of the cost of our gasoline goes to the government.

Thus because of a combination of artificial shortages up and down the distribution pipeline, increasing domestic and foreign demand, and rising taxes, gasoline is set to hit $3.50-$4.00 a gallon this summer.

But we're getting a deal in the US!

In England, petrol now costs $7.25 per US gallon. Over 75% of that is taxes.

We should be thankful.

Now for the good news.

Gasoline, in terms of buying power, really costs less now than it did in 1974. And it takes up less of the average American household budget.

Moreover, gasoline usage accounts for just about 17% of the energy consumed in the United States -- and is falling.

Unlike the relatively free market in oil, the supply of greenbacks in the US is monopoly-controlled by the government. And under government control, things get interesting.

For example, the US government continues to print more money to pay its bills by inflating its way out of its debts. And the government gets to use the newly printed money first, when it has the biggest bang for the buck.

In the US, the Federal Reserve is our central bank. The Fed creates all our money, known by the quaint euphemism "reserves", out of paper and ink and the "full faith and credit" of the US Government. Over the past several years, the Fed has been working day and night with gusto to increase these "reserves"

Since 1973, the dollar has dropped in value by 78%. A gallon of gasoline that costs $3.00 today would have only cost 65¢ then. Perhaps it seems painful because our short-term memories are too good.

But the free market assumes that numbers don't lie. Ask most Americans whether they live in a free-market country and they'd say, sure.

They'd be wrong.

Inflation is reported as running at under 3% in 2007. Unfortunately, the figures were jimmied a few years back to re-write the formula on how inflation is calculated. Official figures say inflation was 3.2% in 2006 -- not counting energy & food.

Other people, however, argue that the real figures may be closer to 7%, depending on whether you count "core" energy prices and who you are and where you live. For the average middle-class commuter suburban family with school-aged children prices certainly feel higher, in spite of the Wal-Mart Effect -- buying ship-loads of aggressively-cheap merchandise from China.

So lots of made-in-America things and services really are getting more expensive -- at least when you price them in ever-weakening dollars. You were right all along. (see: www.nowand-futures.com).

The Real Solution to Cheaper Gas: Increase the supply and cut the demand.

The real solution is straight forward.

1) Drill for more crude oil in America. There's lots there. On the land and in the waters. (The Russians even think that oil's being recreated every day deep down in the earth's crust, and not the result of 200 million year old decaying fossils. But that's another story).

2) Build more new and efficient refineries throughout the country. Stop importing refined petroleum products.

3) Open up more independent gas stations to compete at the retail level.

4) Cut the taxes at all levels, both corporate and excise. Corporate tax is just a pass-through to the consumer anyway (tax to a

company is just another expense to add to their costs; the companies simply raise their selling prices to pay for the taxes).

5) Encourage more companies to enter the oil business as new competitors.

6) Get the government out of the business of over-regulating the marketplace.

7) Create more fuel-efficient and hybrid-energy cars.

8) Establish cheap alternative-energy sources to ease the burden on petroleum product consumption. Electricity generated by state-of-the-art nuclear and clean-burning coal plants comes to mind.

What are the chances of this happening?

Today, quite low. But it ultimately depends on how squeezed the average driver feels. Right now, the pain is not too great and the tradeoffs may not appear so good (will our current amazingly-good US air quality deteriorate?) Ask the question again if and when oil hits $10 a gallon.

Proper implementation of the 8-point strategy could see the 2015 price of gas once again fall below $1 per gallon. But even though cheap energy, driven by oil, helped built the American economic empire of the 20th century, whether this will continue to be perceived as good public policy in the future is unknown.

And what about the stock market? How can the market continue to boom when gas is going through the roof?

Will we see the DJIA crack 15,000 before the election -- or crash and burn below 10,000?

Ronald Reagan once said that an economist is someone who sees something work in practice and wonders whether it will work in theory.

May 30, 2007T

The Goldilocks Economy

Once upon a time there was a stock market in New York. Beginning on May 7, 1792, it used to meet under a Buttonwood tree in lower Manhattan. By March 8, 1817, the New York Stock and Exchange Board, or NYSE had settled down for business. Decades later, in 1882, an enterprising young journalist named Charles Henry Dow created his new Customer's Afternoon Letter. He would later rename it The Wall Street Journal in 1889. Along the way, he also invented the Dow Jones Industrial Average, a handpicked price-weighted collection of the 12 biggest US companies at the time. The time was May 26, 1896. Over the years, the DJIA was expanded by the WSJ editors to represent 30 of America's blue-blood stocks. The movers and shakers that represented the overall American economic machine. The Dow closed on that fateful opening day at 40.96. On Saturday, May 26, 2007, 111 years later, the DJIA stood at 13,507, up 32,977%.

Of course, the DOW was created before the Federal Reserve Board was invented in 1913. Prior to that, booms and busts would occur, but the prices of pretty much everything that Americans consumed tended to stay fairly constant over the decades and centuries. Even stock prices. Before the FED came into being, pretty much everything was traded in pieces of eight, gold and silver coinage.

By the time that World War I came along, the FED was busy pumping out newly minted dollars, but it's real growth period would have to wait for another 25 years until WWII broke out. From the 1940's onwards, there was no looking back, and the FED began cranking out new "liquidity" (econo-speak for money) with abandon. There would never again be a great depression caused by a shortage of ready money. Instead, the spectre of rampant inflation would rule the day. And so it has been ever since.

What does this have to do with the price of the DJIA, or General Electric's stock, or even supermarket-bought eggs, for that matter?

Everything.

As the number of physical and notational dollars in circulation went up, the price of everything denominated in these dollars would rise too. Everything else being equal (and it seldom is), if the number of dollars, say, doubles, but the amount of goods and services produced doesn't, then the price of everything will double as it will take twice as many pieces of paper to but the same thing. Zimbabwe and South America know all about this phenomena - as did the Weimer Republic in pre-Hitler Germany.

Inflation encourages rampant speculation. It drives the bubble mentality, and causes the mis-allocation of investments – along with government tax policy -- by confusing the investor as to what is really going on in a marketplace versus what is happening to the medium of trade -- the currency -- that the transactions are rendered in.

People who buy bonds tend to be wiser and a bit smarter than those folks who buy stocks. At least they tend to be a bit more conservative with their money. They tend to avoid the roller coaster ride of the stock market. They like stable (boring?) returns and the safety in knowing that they get paid before any shareholders do. Especially in bankruptcy court.

Today's bond investors are willing to pay more money to buy a short-term return than they are willing to invest in the long term. The more people buy a bond, the higher its price becomes -- and the lower it's interest payment or yield will be. Whenever the yield inverts, that is, the under-1-year T-Bill pays more interest than, say, the 10-year Treasury note, trouble lies ahead. In just about every instance since WWII, when this has happened, a recession is less than 18 months away. And it's happened in 2007 once again. This means that the savvy bond investors don't see the long-term future through rosy glasses.

And they are usually right.

Then again, there is the 4-year presidential boom-buts cycle well documented by Yale & Jeffery Hirsch and their Stock Trader's Almanac. It seems like the money supply -- and the good times that follow -- seems to grow fairly rapidly just before the presidential elections. And it slows down just afterwards.

This means that whichever party wins in November, 2008, they will likely be facing a serious recession encouraged by falling house prices, retiring baby boomers, tightening money, and a crashing stock market.

Finally, the world is awash with dollars.

Still the dominant global currency -- all commodities from gold to oil to pork bellies are traded in dollars - the US has been printing ever more dollars to pay for its federal budget deficits. These flow into the hands of the people who promptly spend them on Wal-Mart imports from China and overseas oil.

Saudi Arabia and the Asian countries can spend these dollars mostly only in the US. And they are doing so by pouring into the stock and bond and commodity markets. This drives prices up and the cost of running the Federal Government jumps, and the whole cycle repeats itself again. All these fresh dollars can't be spent back in the USA. Some are used by the central banks of other countries as "official reserves" which back up the printing of more Yen, Renminbi, and Rials. This, in turn, drives up inflationary growth in those countries.

A worldwide bubble grows. Eventually, a top will appear. When the overseas investors finally get spooked, they cut back on US stocks and load up on US bonds, backed by the full faith-and-credit of the US government and its 700 overseas military bases in 36 countries. Eventually, they may just want back their own money -- paid in their own currency, driving the dollar down and sending dollar-denominated oil through the roof. High oil prices are an anathema to the stock market. Oil costs permeate everything: food, clothing, manufactured goods. Like a tax, expensive oil raises the costs of doing business. Unlike a tax, there are little offsetting benefits. But the tipping point is still a way off.

In the meanwhile, the stock market should continue to grow and the Goldilocks economy should continue to happen. Enjoy the 14,000 DOW while it lasts. Maybe even 15,000. But don't count on the rest of the 'teens. At least not in the United States. And when the US catches a cold, the rest of the world has historically come down with pneumonia…Of course, like any good economist, I could be completely wrong. And I hope for my sake that I am!

June 5, 2007

Adventures in Global Warming

Once upon a time there was a very mean witch who lived in a sunny and prosperous country which she called Amerika (I don't know why she always spelled it with a 'k', but that's another story...)

She was very angry and very depressed because the vast majority of the citizens of this fair country seemed to be quite happy. And happy is to a wicked witch what oil is to water. (Two other favourite topics we'll return to at a later time...)

To continue. The people lived happy lives with loving families (about 2.3 children on average) in comfortable large houses on leafy green streets in peaceful low-crime neighborhoods that they called suburbs. (Clearly they didn't live in Europe.)

They commuted to work in large safe vehicles (she pejoratively labelled them 'gas guzzlers'). They took vacations by flying all over the place in big shiny jet planes. And they seemed to be having so much fun that just about everyone else in the world wanted to come live with them -- either legally or illegally.

The more these innocent free-loving people seemed to be having fun, the madder the wicked witch became.

Then one day, the wicked witch had a marvellous idea! She could stop these happy souls from having so much fun almost overnight. Why, she could make their lives downright miserable. And better still, she could make them even feel guilty over how they were living their lives. Wow.

She called this great idea "global cooling." Unfortunately, the era was 1975, and the people just laughed her silly thoughts away. Except for Time Magazine, of course. Years went by and she was very depressed indeed. Then, one chilly winter day, she came upon an even better idea to kill off the people's joy. She called her new idea "global warming." And it stuck.

Soon, every wacky politician and populist journalist were knocking on her...

Opps. Wait a minute. I forgot. This article is supposed to be a fair and balanced analysis of the phenomena known as "global warming", and it's economic impact on society. Hmmm...

OK. Here goes.

First, the definitions on how we play this game. The debate over global-warming is done by majority rule. Everyone who believes in global warming caused by humans (it's our fault, folks), raise your hands. OK, as Chairman, I count 110% hands up. Now, comrades, what should we do about it? I know. Let's create a treaty among friends. Majority rules.

We'll hold an expensive meeting of all the rich honest countries and poor corrupt countries on some wealthy overcrowded island where food and oil is imported. We'll meet in Kyoto, Japan. Then, we'll all agree that global warming is our collective fault and the biggest countries causing global warming will have to slash their economies to cut back their emissions of carbon dioxide.

We'll also agree never ever to mention the dirty phrase "global cooling" and the fact that we were all dead wrong 25 years ago. We're right this time for sure. Since God is dead, it's totally our responsibility to manipulate the environment on this planet. We've done a good job in water conservation, ocean fish preservation, elimination of malaria and helping the poor people in Africa break out of poverty. We'll simply use the same tried-and-true collectivist tactics to handle global warming. Damn it. We broke it and we're gonna fix it!

Since the majority of us believe in the slogan "to each according to his needs", we'll create a way of allowing those good countries which don't pollute to sell their spare air to those bad countries which do. We'll exempt the biggest polluters – they're dirt poor you know-- (China, India, Indonesia, Malaysia and Brazil), and we'll blame the most aggressive supporter of clean air & clean water, that shifty fat cat Uncle Sam. Then, we'll spend lots of money on hiring out-of-work scientists to write us made-as-instructed reports proving that global warming is happening -- and that people are the prime cause.

Next, we'll enlist the media -- they don't know anything about science anyway – and we'll use them to smear the tens of thousands of other honest scientists who might object to the questionable science being produced on demand. If we chant the mantra "global warming, global warming" long enough, soon everyone will have read about it in the papers – and you know the papers never lie.

Eventually, if we're really lucky, we'll convert our cause into a cult religion. "Global Warming is the Opiate of the People". You can work wonders with guilt.

We'll pass lots of non-binding resolutions (so the EU countries and our other friends don't have to met their reduction goals). Then we'll call on the United Nations -- where we are solidly in control, brother -- to create an upright honest, respectable Intergovernmental Panel to produce a series of action-item reports, just like we did with the food-for-oil program that worked so well in Iraq.

Finally, we'll make up long-range 50 and 100-year weather forecasts on which to base all our new laws and spending, putting aside the fact that we can't even do accurate 7-day weather forecasts anywhere on the planet yet.

Then we can get filthy rich off of all the wasted human energy, junk science, and corrupt politicians, by creating artificial markets in "emissions trading". We'll have power, prestige, rock music, and guilt-ridden masses obeying our every rule.

Of course, we'll still be flying around in our private jets going to important global warming meetings and using our chauffer-driven limousines to transport us on the diamond lanes (2 people or more, please), and producing pseudo-scientific emotional-manipulating movies showing monster tidal waves and parched deserts. If we play our cards right, we might even get an award or two along the way, maybe even a Noble Peace Prize...

Meanwhile, we'll be able to ignore or suppress the growing number of climatologists, astrophysicists and meteorologists who are saying pesky things like global warming is mostly caused by the sun's periodic heating up, that lots of other planets and moons are getting hotter too, and that the earth has gone through over 30 cold-hot cycles with some much hotter than today.

Since it will take at least a decade -- maybe two or three if we're lucky – to prove us wrong, we can make lots of cash in the meantime.

So, now is the time to stock up on alternative-energy fuels that don't burn carbon. Solar panel technology looks good. And nuclear energy looks great (damn, who let the nukes in here to play?).

For a while we can make money on ethanol -- until we take up so much of it for fuel that our food prices go through the roof and the country gets wise to the fact that it takes more energy to make ethanol that you can get from it. So ethanol production plants, ethanol pipelines, ethanol storage tanks look like good get-rich-quick investments.

And since we have over 1000 years of coal left, investments in new expensive coal burning plants that bury their exhaust gases back underground look promising. As long as oil stays above $60 per barrel. New $3 per gallon gasoline taxes should make sure that the high prices are here to stay. We'll need lots new laws of course. And lots more jails to hold the new global warming criminals.

The bottom line: Global Warming is going to take one heck of a whack out of our economy. It's going to line the pockets of those insiders who can figure out how to play the game, or force other people (us) to pay for it. It's going to drive inflation up and decrease the economy's efficiency the way taxes always do. Global Warming will put America in its place, and bring back that old-time religion of fear and guilt. (But will it save the planet?)

Isn't it all just wonderful, comrade?

June 11, 2007

Government-Controlled Markets Destroy Them

JOIN, or DIE.

The CIA calls it "Blowback". The unintended consequences of one's actions will come back to bite you in the future.

Representative Ron Paul, the only Republican presidential candidate versed in Austrian economics, mentions it in his stump speeches (see www.RonPaul2008.com). George Washington and Dwight Eisenhower warned us about it.

In the political sphere it's fairly obvious. Good deeds can quickly backfire. Support Osama bin Laden with money and weapons to kick the Soviets out of Afghanistan and you've created a monster which will rear up and attack the hand that fed it. Allow illegal immigrants to work off the books for low wages in America and you'll create a potential underclass of law breakers and entitlement seekers. Break Iraq by overthrowing its maniacal dictator and his henchmen, and the vacuum created invites a new group of henchmen to surface.

Economists bemoan the fact that lawmakers at every governmental level are constantly passing laws which look good in the short term -- which are great for reelection vote-getting -- but have unexpected long-term negative effects.

In physics, Isaac Newton observed that for every action there is an equal and opposite reaction. When lawmakers spend the peoples' money, the law of economics is much worse. Because of the entitlement effect, monetary expansion, and inflation indexing, the delayed reaction can compound to orders of magnitude.

Here are a few examples.

For nearly 100 years, the Federal Government accumulated a mountain hoard of silver. Over the next century, Washington proceeded to sell off this national treasure at a weekly fixed price which was under the real production cost. In the end, silver was artificially pegged at $1.29 per ounce. Then, one day in 1967 they ran out of silver and stopped selling. Almost overnight, the price of silver jumped to $5, as the market acknowledged that for years the cost of mining silver was far higher than the government's selling price.

Soon, people discovered that their silver dimes, quarters, half-dollars and dollars were worth more melted down than as coins in their pockets. Within a few months, America ran out of species, and the government was forced to abandon the centuries-old tradition of providing real money for circulation.

The silver coins were replaced with base-metal clad coins, and the inviolate promise printed on the dollar bill (the old "silver certificate") -- to redeem the paper note for real silver money at the government bank -- was eliminated. The price of silver briefly (over)shot, up to $50 per ounce, as the marketplace reacted to the release of the government control over the silver price. Gresham's Law (bad money drives out the good) was proven true once again.

The principle at work is simple: whenever a government manipulates a market -- in either direction -- the market will be distorted. Eventually it will break free from its bonds, and a new market-based equilibrium price will be established. The longer the government distorts the marketplace, the greater the reaction will be.

Milk prices illustrate the opposite phenomena. Government price-fixing keeps the price of milk artificially high with minimum selling price regulations and support payments. Farmers, seeing they can make good money in this government-manipulated food industry, over-invest and over-produce milk.

The result? Excessive milk production is sometimes poured down the drain and mountains of milk power and milk products build up. To get rid of these, the government ships the milk over-seas to African and other under-developed countries to help feed their starving citizens.

This, in turn, destroys the local dairy industries which can't compete with the free milk being sent by the Americans, and countless local dairies are wiped out. This process was discussed in the Bible. Except, of course, the opposite course of action was recommended: don't give the needy free fish but rather teach them how to become fishermen. A free ride always creates a "moral hazard" as they say in econospeak.

An initially virtuous circle created from innocent good intentions thus segues into a viciously destructive one.

And so it goes over and over again. A well-meaning effort which distorts the natural free market at work usually backfires down the road.

Take the government's creation of Medicare Part D -- the "free drugs" benefit. Originally conceived as a safety net for poorer people above 65, it was quickly expanded into an entitlement program for all older Americans, from Billionaires on down. The cost of the program? Perhaps trillions of dollars over the next century. Who really knows?

Of course, future Americans can't pay this bill, any more than they can pay their looming Social Security bill. But Social Security is not counted "on the books" as an expense obligation of the US Government -- the way any corporation must do under the law. Thus the staggering future liabilities remain invisible.

The solutions are obvious: either the government repudiates its debt, or it breaks its promise to pay in more subtle ways. It will raise the retirement age, tax Social Security payments, and stop SS indexing. It will inflate the money supply to pay for the future bill with more pieces of paper worth less and establish "means testing" for wealthier citizens. Eventually the problem will be fixed, but at a much higher cost in dollars and heartache.

Then there's the process of shipping our hard-earned wealth overseas to buy oil and cheap commodities from mostly totalitarian regimes unfriendly to our American values of individual freedom and liberty.

Why? Because it is politically expedient to drill for oil any-where else other than our own backyard. And it is politically ex-pedient to destroy the old-line manufacturing industries in North America (including Mexico) to feed the consumer's thirst for cheap goods, no questions asked.

But, once again, for every action there is a reaction -- and usually unexpected. The mountain of overseas dollars are now washing back onto our shores. And they are buying real goods and commodities, real estate and company shares. They are not buying the Government's T-bills and bonds they way they did just a few months ago.

The result? Bond prices have dropped sharply, interest rates are rising, and the FED is caught between a rock and a hard place as it rides the roller coaster over the next few years. And so are we. Everything should become a lot more expensive in the process as the glut of dollars drives up prices. This includes rare Picasso's and publicly-traded stocks. Just don't call this phenomena inflation.

The message should be simple -- and obvious. Whenever any government tampers with the free market, there will be hell to pay -- eventually.

June 26, 2007

Got Milk?

JOIN, or DIE.

So what's the price of milk got to do with The Adventures of Jonathan Gullible: A Free Market Odyssey?

On Sunday, July 1st, 2007, the California Department of Food and Agriculture raised the minimum retail price for a gallon of low-fat milk to $3.10, compared to $2.10 in January, up 48%. The state sets the "lowest reported lawful retail price" for milk; the law says milk cannot be sold below what the state decides. Or else. Just like the old USSR price fixing boards.

The state government reports this is really good for farmers. They forgot to say it is really bad for consumers. In fact, Kelly Krug, director of the "Division of Marketing" of the CDFA was saddened that they were forced to do it: "If it were a totally free market, the trading of these commodities could translate into the (figure) that farmers get," said Krug.

Huh?

In a totally free market a gallon of milk would probably be selling for under $1.00.

It's clear that Mr. Krug never learned how the free market-place works when he was growing up. But it's not surprising.

Economics can be confusing. Especially if you are in high school. Even more so if you are in college.

Most kids start out living -- in economists' terms -- the fine socialist life. They don't have to cook or feed themselves. They don't have to buy their own clothes. Many even get a free weekly allowance -- just for being alive. Sometimes their parents open a bank savings account for them. They have their own cell phones, I-

Pods, computers and digital cameras -all usually bought for them by their parents. And when they become teenagers, they often are given their own credit cards (guaranteed, of course, by their parents).

The lucky few get part-time jobs as weekend shop clerks or doing paper deliveries, but many teenagers never experience the opportunity to work for a living until they finally graduate from college many years later.

It's then that the rubber hits the road. Having been raised to be on the dole (though, by then, having become expert consumers) they are woefully unprepared to deal with the real world of economics, only willing to pay them for their talents in a competitive job marketplace.

So it comes as a shock that socialist ideas don't count for much in a free-market world (unless they get a government job). Concepts like accountability for one's actions, supply and demand, cost versus price, and time versus money are often unknown. And the even stranger notion that you have to give something first before you can take something back is hard to fathom. The old Soviet joke: "they pretend to pay us and we pretend to work", while tellingly funny is, in fact, backwards in describing how the marketplace really works. The free market rewards those the highest who can provide the most value.

When they get their first pay check the reality settles in. It's then that they see how much money is taken out, bit by bit, from their gross income for their take home pay. Items like social security, Medicare, health insurance, unemployment insurance, workman's comp, federal income tax, state income tax and (sometimes) city income tax become instantly – painfully -- obvious on their pay check stub. Most of these costs are, of course, forced subsidies which take the money out of their pockets to transfer it to the benefit of others. Hidden expenses like the employer's matching payments to social security, Medicare & the insurance programs don't even enter their mind.

Wouldn't it be nice if someone would just write a book, in

a humorous sort of way, which could gently teach them the basic economic principles that make the world work while they are still, say, in grade school or high school?

Fortunately my friend Ken Schoolland has written such a book. It's been translated into over 40 foreign languages, read by hundreds of thousands of kids in dozens of countries, and can be downloaded as an English-language edition, complete with commentary for the college-level student. It's called The Adventures of Jonathan Gullible, and is available for free at www.JonathanGullible.com.

Jonathan, is an adventuresome soul who gets lost one day in a great storm while sailing near his seaside town. He winds up crashing into a shallow reef of a mysterious island which, he later discovers, the locals call "Currumpo".

Along the way, he meets the people in their various villages and discovers, with great innocence, a world turned upside down. One day while wondering into one particular town, he sees a dignified, well-dressed man kneeling in the street, trying painfully to walk. Jonathan offers him a hand. "No thank you, said the man wincing in pain. I can walk OK. Using knees takes some time getting used to. It's a minor adjustment to the tax code. The Council of Lords decided that tall people have too many advantages. We're taxed in direct proportion to our height." Jonathan was dumbstruck: "you'll walk on your knees for a tax break?" "Sure, replied the man in a pained voice. Our whole lives are shaped to fit the tax code. There are some who have even started to crawl!"

Jonathan's adventures carry him to a corrupt printer at "the Official Bureau of Money Creation" where he learns about the profits of official counterfeiting and he meets a young farmer woman whose farm was taken away by the Farm Police for producing too much food. He talks with a fisherman who can no longer fish in his favorite lake, ruined by pollution. When Jonathan asks: "why do others take your fish and dump trash in the lake, the fisherman responds, oh no, this isn't my lake. It belongs to everyone -- just like the forests and the streams. It's run by the Council of Lords. They appoint a manager and pay him from my taxes. The fish manager is supposed to watch out for too much fish and dumping. Funny thing is, friends of the Lords get to fish and dump as they please".

Jonathan later flees just in time from "The Democracy Gang", a group of thugs who "surround anyone they find and they vote on what to do with them." He's told: "they take their money, lock 'em in a cage, or force 'em to join their gang. When the gang first attacked people, the police hauled them into court for their crimes. The gang argued that they were following majority rule, same as the law. Votes decide everything – legality, morality, everything! The judges ruled three to two in their favor: 'Divine Right of Majorities' they called it."

And so it goes until Jonathan can make his escape back to reality.

In 39 short chapters Professor Schoolland (who teaches economics and political science at Hawaii Pacific University) gently carries the reader through all the major principles of a free market-based society by pointing out the absurdities of a corrupt socialist system. It seems to work.

Although written for the high school student, it's not too advanced for a government bureaucrat to read. Mr. Krug, you can still download a copy for yourself - before the price of milk gets fixed at $4 a gallon in California.

July 5, 2007

United States Debt and the World

JOIN, or DIE.

At last count, the United States owes the rest of the world over two trillion dollars. That's two thousand billion dollars, a lot of money even for the late Senator Everett Dirksen. As recently as the 1970's, America was the major creditor nation, lending money overseas and investing its dollars abroad. We were exporting food, airplanes, technology and even consumer goods. In those days, the total of all imports to and exports from the US to the rest of the world amounted to slightly less than 12% of its GDP. And almost half of that was trade between the US and Canada and Mexico.

But no more. Over the past 3 decades, the US has bought far more goods than it has sold. And those goods now are sold to America from factories in China, the far east and South America, as well as massive amounts of oil from Venezuela and the other OPEC countries. The current monthly balance of trade deficit is running at about $58 billion. China alone reports to have over $1 trillion in US money in its coffers. And our total foreign trade has risen to above a quarter of our adjusted GDP.

So, this is really bad for the US, right? Not necessarily. At least not in the short-term and perhaps not even in the long term. Here's the reasoning.

China, and the other exporters to the US, have been willing to play the role of a modern Mercantilist -- as if the defunct Mercantile system of the 17th century was somehow still alive. (see Wikipedia for a good definition of Mercantilism and why it failed.) But mercantilism was based on seizing a positive balance-of-trade (one exports more than one imports), tariff protectionism, and the accumulation of foreign lucre in the form of real money, i.e. gold bullion. In these post-Bretton Woods (floating currencies), post-1971 (Nixon cancels dollar convertibility; no more gold standard) and post WTO-treaty (no tariff or price-fixing) days, none of this applies.

So, China and Saudi Arabia continue to ship real wealth into the United States in the form of plasma TV's, baby toys, seafood and energy, and in return accept pieces of paper called dollars. More usually, of course, they take electronic computer notations entered onto the electronic books of central banks. The result is that the rest of the world has been massively subsidizing the standard of living of American citizens so that they could keep their own factories and plants working -- and citizens from overthrowing their often despotic regimes.

Now the problem becomes, what do these foreign countries do with this mountain of US dollar-dominated electronic IOU's?

Ultimately, popular wisdom says they have to return them back to the United States -- where they can spend them on buying goods and services here.

Well, they've already done that.

But the US dollar accounts for 67% of the world's reserve currency, and the US economy, with 5% of the world's population, represents over 1/3rd of the world's GDP. Suddenly bringing back all of those dollars to the US would be a tough go here. Inflation would soar and import prices would go through the roof as these extra dollars flooded the domestic market. The dollar, of course, would immediately fall, making our exports far cheaper to buy abroad -- if there were any buyers left.

But it would be a disaster overseas. Country after country would collapse into depression as hundreds of millions of workers would suddenly find their factories no longer able to export profitably to US consumers.

So let's pretend you are the central banker in charge of China today. What can you do with your trillion dollars right now? First, you can buy lots of US T-bills from the American treasury. Fortunately, now that the US Government needs to fund its half-trillion dollar deficit created by fighting the Iraq war, you can once again buy 30-year treasury notes. But their yield is terrible: under 5% right now, and perhaps headed lower.

Being a prudent banker (lest you be shot) you only buy several hundred billion dollars worth of T-bills. Of course, you keep several hundred billion dollars in your electronic vault to use as "reserves" to back the several hundred billion Renminbi (the "people's currency") you've printed to pay for all those new domestic factories and high-rise Shanghai condos the developers are building.

Next, you start buying commodities on the world's markets. Fortunately, all the commodities you want happen to be denominated in dollars on the world's commodity exchanges. Great! So you buy concrete, steel, aluminum, oil, gold and silver. The prices shoot up but you've been able to get rid of another several hundred billion dollars. Then you start buying American companies like seaports (Long Beach), computer manufacturers (IBM PC Division) and oil companies (Conoco) -- whoops -- that last one is deemed "strategic" by the US government and they won't let you do it.

Then you slowly allow your currency to move upwards viz-a-viz the US dollar -- it's undervalued at least 58% per the Economist's Big Mac standard so as not to scare the US markets.

Next, you convert your dollar hoard into Yen, Euros, Pounds and Swiss Francs. Again very slowly so as to let the air out of the US dollar very gradually. The UK £ breaks $2 to 1 and the € jumps to almost $1.40 but the world goes on.

Finally, you start investing in the US and global stock markets. Through your subsidiary pension funds (which are much less transparent than your central bank holdings) and the world's private hedge funds (such as Blackstone) you start buying public equities and corporate debt. The stock markets explode in growth as a result.

Problem. What do you do with the next trillion dollars you make over the next 10 years? Suggestion: buy sub-par US mortgage debt. There will be a lot on the table for sale. And since ultimately you really can't spend all those dollars outside of the US forever, eventually you'll have to buy "Made-in-the-USA" goods and services. At least that's how the theory goes.

Either that or face the consequences: the world needs the US a lot more than the US appears to need the world. If it has to, the US treasury could limit the overseas dollar repatriation at any time. Even France made the Franc unconvertible in the early 1980's. After all, only 22% of total US GDP is foreign trade, and a third of that is with Canada and Mexico -- and they're safely inside the NAFTA free-trade zone. Rest assured that this "nuclear option" contingency has been well simulated at the Treasury.

The best solution? Keep all of those dollars safely tucked at home, and use them as reserves to print more Yuan/Renminbi. That way we all inflate world-wide at the same Fed-controlled rate, just like our banks do here inside the US. Giving up your central bank sovereignty to the US Federal Reserve Bank is better than losing your head! All the world's currencies have become fiat currencies anyway, backed only by the "full faith and credit" of their respective governments. Of course I could be wrong.

August 28, 2007

Of Traveler's Checks, Green Stamps, & Little Iron Men

Back in 1896, the Sperry and Hutchinson Company (S&H to you readers over 50) invented the concept of the "loyalty program". For over a century, millions of consumers collected these 'free' stamps which were handed out by retailers. After pasting hundreds of them in a book (which took years), they could be exchanged at special redemption centers for 'free' list-price merchandise.

Eight years earlier, in 1891, J.C. Fargo, then president of American Express, had invented the Travelers' Check -- as a way of minimizing the risk of carrying cash which could be lost or stolen. You'd hand over your money to American Express in exchange for a fancy-looking IOU which they would redeem from the merchant you paid in the distant future. Before long, American Express travelers checks were circulating throughout the world as cash themselves -- and a lot safer than their own often-worthless currencies.

J.C. was the younger brother of co-founder William Fargo who with Henry Wells, after creating American Express in 1850, went on to found Wells Fargo & Co. in 1852. They were an industrious lot of financiers back in those days.

But back to our story.

During its heyday in the 1960's, S&H was printing three times more stamps than the US Post Office. People were collecting them by the shopping cart full. The enormously successful S&H Green Stamps marketing ploy was followed by American Airlines which, with a slight twist, invented the world's first Frequent Flier program on May Day, 1981. No humor was likely intended.

In the 90's, savvy retailers began to issue mail-in rebates with the same effect. A product which would other wise sell for, say, $50 could be marketed for $20 with a $30 rebate. PMA, a US marketing firm, estimated that in 2005 alone, $486 million worth of rebates were redeemed, but that this represented only 21% of rebate-eligible sales.

Meanwhile, for over a century, American Express has been printing billions of dollars (and pounds, yen, marks and a dozen other currencies) of traveler's checks annually.

What's all this have to do with the price of dollars -- or more importantly, of the greenbacks themselves?

Well, basically, all these schemes - including the printing of almost a trillion dollars of greenbacks - involve three things: 1) they are all forms -- directly or indirectly -- of creating money out of thin air, 2) they all rely on the good "faith and credit" of the issuer to ultimately repay the debts -- in the future -- that these various IOU's in the form of stamps, checks & 'little iron men' represent, and 3) they all count on a little-known but well-cherished fact: lots of green stamps, travelers checks and US dollars are never actually cashed in or redeemed or deposited. Ever.

Wow! What a 'float' for a loan. The terms to the borrower (S&H, Amex, the Treasury) are: zero interest and no repayment -- forever! They are all, of course, fiat currencies. And this process has made most similar debt-instrument issuers very wealthy indeed.

Every time an airliner crashes somewhere, hundreds of thousands, perhaps millions of dollars of travelers checks are never cashed. Periodic wars which blow up houses and people blow up their greenbacks as well. Millions of little old ladies with dresser drawers bulging with half-full books of green stamps never turned them in for that proverbial toaster. And we all know about the billions of air miles we've collected -- but are unable to redeem. In fact, if all the air miles were actually converted to free flights with the airlines, the entire airline industry would collapse into bankruptcy.

The economists have a word to describe this funny money business when it comes to currencies issued by a central bank. They call it seigniorage. Since the US dollar is no longer backed by anything of real value, such as gold or silver species, some wags have called this process a Ponzi Scheme. But they would be wrong.

Ponzi was on the hook for 100% of the IOU's he issued.

The US economy represents 35% of the world's GDP. But as most commodity and other global transactions (bond issuance, corporate finance, etc.) are conducted in dollars, the US benefits from the fact that hundreds of billions of physical dollars are circulating overseas – and many if not most of these will never find their way back home.

This means that the U.S. Treasury can print up far more dollars than it otherwise would have to pay back. This, in turn, makes the US dollar a unique currency among the world's currencies.

But wait, it gets better. The US government creates a far-greater amount of electronic IOU's (T-bills and the like), most of which are shipped overseas to pay for our import balance of trade deficit. Like the actual greenbacks, these other dollars can circulate outside the US for years; they are often retained in the bank coffers of other central banks which hold them as "reserves" to back up their own money printing. This dollar hegemony provides an immediate boost to the real GDP of the US economy itself. Estimates range around 1% plus or minus for the 'float' benefit we get inside the USA.

Lots of other countries would, of course, like to be in the same position. Not a chance.

But there is one up-and-comer which might challenge the American printing press in the future: the European Union and its Euro, another fiat currency. But can they pull it off? It looks remotely possible.

As the US continues to print more paper dollars and create

even more electronic debt (the FED calls it 'liquidity') to pay its bills, it has passed off a mountain of dollars onto the rest of the world. And if they ever really start handing them back to the US it would drive inflation up the wall inside the US and crash the world's economy for everyone else.

A more likely scenario is a long-term slowly-declining dollar viz-a-viz the Euro.

The camel's nose is now firmly under the tent. Whether the Euro can challenge the US dollar for its coveted global currency position remains to be seen. But I wouldn't bet against the full faith and credit – and military might and entrepreneurial creativity -- of the US just yet, no matter how much Charles Ponzi must be rolling in his grave at the thought of such an opportunity lost.

The bottom line: in international finance as in the new world order it pays to be on top. If you owe the bank $1 million, it owns you. If you owe the bank $1 trillion, you own it - and the world is America's banker. Or, put another way, you can have your cake and eat it too if you are the world's money hedgemon. No wonder the EU wants to muscle in on the US turf with its new-fangled Euro. Wouldn't you?

September 19, 2007

Social Security, Ponzi Schemes and Moral Hazards

JOIN, or DIE.

Economists call it "moral hazard": an idea that originated in the insurance industry. Simply put, moral hazard arises when one party in an economy can pass off the risk of his actions/behaviors to another. This process distorts the natural marketplace, enabling that person to take more risks than would otherwise be prudent, knowing that the consequences would be borne by someone else.

A simple example. International banks over-aggressively lend money to spendthrift countries. When the inevitable financial panic occurs, the International Monetary Fund (IMF) often steps in to cover the poor banks' losses. This action bails the banks out of their foolish positions -- and perpetuates the corrupting cycle in the future.

Insurance, when properly "underwritten" (i.e. "sold" to you and me) by the insurer, does not trigger moral hazard. Take life insurance. Or what should better be called "death insurance." You bet you are going to die; the insurance company bets you are going to live. In the aggregate the insurance company can calculate the overall average death statistics for a large group of customers quite accurately. A good profit can be made based on the fact that your chance of dying early will be countered by the vast majority of the other average-life-expectancy policy holders.

Knowing that your family is now fully covered if you die prematurely, you might be willing to take greater risks than usual, perhaps driving a bit too fast, or taking up the hobby of skydiving from airplanes, or taking extended holidays in war zones. But it is unlikely that you will actually do so. And insurance companies have become quite good at excluding individuals who attempt to "game the system", such as those who have terminal cancer but don't reveal their condition.

Which brings us to the problem of government insurance schemes. And in particular, government insurance schemes which do not protect the insurer -- the government --against possible moral hazards of the insured. In other words, Social Security, Medicare, Medicaid and ERISA (defaulting private insurance retirement programs that are back stopped by the US government). Here, the Federal Government guarantees that the insurance schemes will always pay out, no matter how expensive the cost becomes or how clever the system can be gamed by individuals succumbing to moral hazard.

Since these schemes are really government promises made by politicians over time to capture the favor of specific voting groups -- and thereby get re-elected to office -- no simple checks-and-balances mechanism exists to prevent a moral hazard from being created. This is especially true when the benefit (the money) flows from the government to mostly third party beneficiaries, such as hospitals, health care professionals, drug manufacturers, and trade union bosses. No wonder, then, that the largest and most powerful lobby group in the US today is no longer the National Rifle Association. It's AARP (which used to stand for the American Association of Retired Persons). AARP now has well over 60 million members, and is growing larger as each baby boomer turning 50 becomes eligible to join.

Of course, Social Security, Medicare, Medicaid and ERISA are not really true insurance programs. Unlike legitimate privately-run insurance companies, there is no reserve pool of assets to tap into when needed to pay out to future beneficiaries. The money collected in premiums is not used for investments, it's simply used to immediately pay the current bills of earlier insured people. Contrary to what a former national politician once alleged, there (alas) is no "lock box" with a treasure trove of assets safely tucked away in the government vaults. What really exists is yet another Ponzi scheme this time made legal by government definition.

One way the politicians can successfully pull this confidence trick off is to simply hide the real numbers from the public's eyes. It's easy. These debts owing to future claimants are never put on the books. Nowhere in the multi-trillion dollar US budget will you find the tens (hundreds?) of trillions of dollars of unfunded Social Security, Medicare, Medicaid, etc. debts owed by the federal government. They ain't there.

Generation X and Generation Y, being somewhat smarter than the baby boomers, cottoned on to this a while back. They fully expect the US government to renege on its overly-ambitious obligations. This renouncing has already started. Full SS payments used to start at 65. It's now, 66 or 67 -- depending on how young you now are. Expect the payout age to be raised to 70 in the not too distant future... The payments used to be tax free. Now 50% are taxed above certain incomes. Expect that to be raised to 100% -- and cut off completely for people above a certain gross retirement income. It WILL happen.

Eventually, almost no one will qualify to receive any Social Security benefits. That's the only way the government can extract itself from the moral hazard risk it has fallen prey to. By the way, Congress has historically exempted itself from paying into the Social Security system. It has a much nicer and juicier plan for its own members. It also allows most government employees from opting out of SS as well -- and into privately-run retirement and health plans like the State of California's CALPERS program.

Medicare and Medicaid programs are next in line for moral hazard duty and government "adjustments" to counter the moral hazards created in the first place.

So my best advice for every private "investor" in these government insurance schemes? Avoid ever putting your money into them in the first place, or find ways of getting your money out as fast as you can -- preferably before the next "beneficiary." But here's an even better solution. Get a good government job. Preferably as a university economics professor at a state-owned college.

September 28, 2007

The European Union as Humpty Dumpty

JOIN, or DIE.

From the beginning, tiny Belgium has been at the very core of the European Union nee European Community nee European Economic Community nee European Coal Board. It was one of the 'Original Five' countries which created the EU's predecessor trade body in the early 50's.

Over the decades, Belgium has changed quite a bit.

With each new treaty came new laws, new regulations, and new bureaucracies. Eventually a strange 3-headed monster appeared, being part democratic -- the European Parliament, and part bureaucratic: the unelected Executive branch, run by a committee and which is called the European Commission.

Brussels grew from a tiny city to a sprawling metropolis that looks much like Washington, D.C., complete with giant office buildings bulging with outside consultants and lobbyists. It seems strangely familiar.

Belgium in some ways reflects internally what a multi-cultural, multi-linguistic, multi-government beast the EU has become. Charged originally with the sole task of lowering certain commodity tariffs among its members, the original European adventure in free trade has morphed into a political union with its own currency, and soon, its own foreign policy and its own foreign embassies. There will be a new EU President too.

This is scheduled to happen by 2009 as soon as the new 'non-constitution' constitutional treaty takes effect.

So far, none of the 27 EU countries have decided to call a referendum to allow their citizens to vote on creating this new superstate. Only Ireland will submit the 2007 'Lisbon Treaty' to a popular vote. But only because its own constitution requires it.

It's just as well. Polls in half a dozen countries, especially including the United Kingdom, show that the non-constitution constitutional treaty would be voted down handily.

Democratic voting rights issues and minority groups scrabbling in Belgium spells Trouble at the heart of the EU -- which at its heart is an essentially non-democratic top-down commissar-structured organization. Over the years its legitimacy has continued to drop. Once again -- just last week -- the 13th annual audit of the EU books by the European Audit Court has flunked a passing grade. Lots of money has been misplaced by the raging EU bureaucracy.

It seems like Belgium has been rather successfully operating for the past 6 months without a central government for itself. The French and Flemish parts of the country aren't speaking to each other. And now the pressure is increasing on them to split up into two separate new nation states. While that is unlikely at this point, once again the observation that all political power is ultimately local may be proven true.

If the EU loses its momentum to push to "ever closer union", it's possible that some of the nation states will start spinning off to the outer edges -- a la centrifugal force at work.

And at the edge of the EU is the EFTA: the European Free Trade Area. EFTA, as it turns out, actually works quite well. It has stayed true to its original design as a free trade area. And it currently consists of real rich countries like Iceland, Switzerland, Norway and Lichtenstein. It has all the same free trade and open borders benefits between its members and the EU -- but is far more independent of Brussels -- and the EU central bank and Euro.

So why would anyone want to be in the "new improved" EU hankering to open up its own foreign embassies and apply its ever-expanding veto over formerly sovereign member nations?

If you scan the crystal ball for a realistic EU future, could you see, for example, a German general in charge of the French and/or English nuclear arsenals? Or a German banker in charge of all financial decisions of the now-subservient nation states? Remember, the European Central Bank is located in Frankfurt, not Paris or London.

Then there is the possibility of a single foreign minister controlling all EU foreign policy. From Paris, of course.

Back in the British Isles, the Scot-controlled Labor Party unleashed a slowly-growing monster in their decade in power in Westminster. As a result, the pressure is mounting north of the English border for Scotland to succeed from the UK and apply under EU rules to be admitted as a new independent country. You can count on this happening within the next 10 years -- maybe less. (You've heard it here first).

They will then join the United Nations with their own seat, and create their own foreign ministry and military. But how will England and Scotland divvy up the military bases in Scotland? This matter -- along with the "Scottish" oil will be relatively easily resolved. England (the UK) will retain its nuclear capability and Security Council seat. In return, England will agree not to veto Scotland's entry into the EU.

One island over, Northern Ireland -- after the next census in 2011 -- will likely swing to majority Catholic population (they have more babies than Protestants) -- and most likely will vote to merge with the now wealthier (!) Eire. (Thanks to truckloads of German monies).

The rump UK, consisting of England and Wales will immediately be dominated by the Conservatives -- who will no longer be forced to subsidize the Scots from south of the border as they've been doing for decades now.

While Scotland and N. Ireland will immediately adopt the Euro, England will stay with the Pound -- and most likely vote to remove itself from the EU and rejoin the EFTA.

If this happens, count on at least five other EU countries also leaving the EU and joining EFTA. These include several of the Baltic states, several other Eastern European states - who have discovered that Brussels -- without the German money -- is beginning to look a lot like their former task masters in Moscow. Turkey would successfully join the EFTA, not the EU.

So any weakening in the EU fabric -- however slight -- will be perceived by the Brussels as a threat to the group unity and a sign to those at the edges (like the UK) that there can be a break-up process which would provide a better more democratic method of home governance and group hugs.

When the threat to the EU polity comes from Brussels, the near city-state at the very heart of the EU, this is indeed a big deal in the power brokers and bureaucrats offices throughout the EU (and who work mostly in Brussels itself).

Picture Washington, D.C. deciding that it will become an independent state and not a vassal of the U.S. federal government. Impossible? Perhaps. But only because the US constitution is real: the European Union's constitution-cum-treaty lacks that one essential characteristic.

November 21, 2007

You Can Blame Herman Hollerith for the Sub-Prime Meltdown

JOIN, or DIE.

It's become popular for the current crowd in Congress to try and find a scapegoat to blame for the sub-prime real estate loan meltdown. You should forget the lack of proper risk analysis of securitized loan packages by the bond rating agencies. Also ignore the lack of standards in making decent loans by the banks and mortgage brokers. With all that cheap money sloshing around just waiting to be lent what would you expect?

In the desire to help our liberal colleagues solve this painful problem, it is necessary to trace this particular history back to its roots.

Several decades ago, an extraordinarily popular BBC/PBS series was presented by the science writer James Burke. He called it Connections, and the first series' 7 episodes neatly tied together dozens of historic inventions -- like gunpowder and the telegraph -- which have brought us the modern world of thermonuclear devices and the internet.

We can easily do the same thing with Herman Hollerith and his amazing invention, the computer punch card.

Dr. Hollerith was a mathematician in the 1880's who had been hired by the US government to automate the 1890 census. The prior census had taken nearly a decade to complete, and the process was still being done by walk-about census takers using quill pen and paper.

Dr. Hollerith was familiar with the Jacquard loom, an 18th century invention which had automated the weaving of fabrics. The Jacquard system used a series of wooden boards with holes punched into them at strategic locations. As these wooden boards, which were looped together with a series of cords, passed through the loom, wooden pegs or fingers would fit into the holes and cause the machinery to duplicate the weaving pattern.

Hollerith used the idea of Charles Babbage and his punch-card driven mechanical tabulator to create his prototype "punch card". The new punch card was cut from a thick piece of paper to be the same size as the 1887 dollar bill. There was originally room for just 24 columns of data, but each column could be punched in 12 different positions using a round hole punch. Hollerith selected the dollar bill size of 3.25 by 7.375 inches for his cards because he used the Treasury Department boxes as containers.

One column was used for the person's sex, another two for their age, and so on. And two were reserved for the year: 90 would mean 1890, 00 would mean 1900.

By the 1950's, modern computers and the Cobol and Fortran programming languages had codified the date field to two digits. Programmers were aware that there might be a problem around the turn of the next century, in the year 2000. But that was half a century away, and everyone would be long gone by then, and surely the problem would be fixed.

By 1995, US industry had awoken to its worst nightmare.

By 1998 it was in full panic mode. Hundreds of billions of dollars were being spend by the Fortune 1000 companies to repair the global network of computers -- all of which were keyed to 2 digit years -- and which tests had shown would lock up and stop functioning at the stroke of midnight, 1999.

No electricity, no dial-tone, no water or sewage, no banking or airline service was projected by scores of computer experts. Years of IT budgets were spent in a few months. Internet routers were scrapped and new equipment, new operating systems, and new programs had to be written to eliminate what came to be known as the Y2K bug. An explosion in growth in the high tech computer and telecoms fields was the result.

Technology stocks doubled then tripled. Some went up by 1000%.

The Fed was concerned, if not frightened. Y2K could potentially lock up the entire financial system of the United States, if not the world. By the closing weeks of 1999, it was excessively pumping hundreds of billions of newly printed dollars into ATM machines nationwide, and truckloads of currency were shipped to the 12 regional Federal Reserve Banks.

Almost overnight, the M1 money supply shot through the roof.

By February, 2000, it was clear that the worst was over. The bullet had been dodged. And the Fed began to pull back its oversupply of money that was no longer needed.

The money supply shrunk just as fast as it had been expanded during the crisis. By the summer, however, it became clear that something was deeply troubling in the high tech field. All the predicted new spending on high technology had already been taken from future corporate and government budgets. It had all been spend several years before. The order books dried up. Companies began to lay off thousands of people. The stock market tanked, and the famous "dot com" bubble collapsed.

Now a new panic was felt at the Fed. And when 911 happened, the panic became compounded. As the economy began to sag, the Fed needed to act to stimulate it back into activity. It did so by progressively lowering its interest rates month after month for almost two years, until the cost to borrow money for prime lenders was only 1% -- way below the annual inflation rate.

The result, coupled with the Bush tax cut and immediate infusion of tax rebates, kick-started the economy into overdrive. The US bounced from a sure recession to a sure boom -- and the boom was driven by cheap money flowing into both the stock market and the housing sector. With so much money available and begging to be lent, banks were eager to issue mortgages to anyone who barely qualified -- and many who didn't.

"Don't ask, don't tell" loans (known as "no docs" -- no proof of income, no tax returns needed) exploded. Super cheap ARMS -- in particular short term teaser rate loans that would reset their interest rates upwards in two or three years hence, beginning around 2007 -- jumped from 5% to 75% of loans issued in some markets.

The result is evident today. We're in a real mess. And the end is not yet in sight. As the baby boomers begin to retire in earnest and cash out their market investments, coupled with a desire to downsize their "McMansions", the real estate market could continue to unwind for years. Serious property readjustment in previous bubbles (ala Japan, South America, the UK) has seen values drop by 15% to 30% or more.

If there is a moral to this story, it is that the Fed over-reacted in the fall of 1999 and again in the fall of 2001. The market whipsaw was the result. But what was the Fed to do? After all, that is its job, to control the nation's money supply by increasing or decreasing the amount of fiat money in circulation and to set the interest rates that the banking system charges lenders.

Turning over this most important of the free market's products -- the creation and supply of money -- to the government-controlled monopoly of the Federal Reserve Board back in 1913 may yet turn out to be the most profoundly disastrous policy decision that the Congress has ever made in a long line of foolish experiments with socialism and government manipulation of the free market.

As a property owner, I hope that my analysis is wrong. Massive future inflation may yet bail out the home owner's nominal loss valuation. Time will tell. Anyway, you can tell Congress that it's all Herman Hollerith's fault.

November 27, 2007

How the Fed Pulled the Rabbit out of the Hat

The week of November 25, 2007 may go down in history as the week that the Federal Reserve did the seemingly impossible: stabilize the black hole which is the sub-prime meltdown, halt the continual erosion of the dollar versus the Euro, Pound and Yen, encourage overseas investors to come pouring back into the bargain dollar investment market, decimate the inflation rate, knock down the gold price, drive the DOW up over 500 points in 2 days, and push the Republicans up in the online Zogby Poll to beat Hillary Clinton.

Okay, so maybe the Fed wasn't responsible for all of the above. But the bottom line remains that, suddenly, the financial world seems to be looking a lot better. While some would argue that this is a sucker's market (and they may still be correct), the truth is that the Fed did some pretty tricky things a few months ago that appear to be beginning to bear fruit.

The most important tweak was barely covered by the financial press and not at all by the major national newspapers. I was first tipped off to this by Dr. Gary North.

On August 17, the Fed published a change to its regulations "clarifying" the overnight borrowing of funds from the Fed by the nation's major banks, the so-called "repo" or repurchase agreements. The Fed now allows for "a broad range of collateral".

The Fed specifically said: "The Reserve Banks accept performing mortgages. This could include sub-prime mortgages." Wow!

The Federal Reserve decided to allow the banks to present as security to the Fed the banks' doggy portfolio of sub-prime loans -- worthless in the open market -- and treat them as if they worth fully 100% of their face value, not their market value. Moreover, the Fed allowed the banks to maintain these loans not just for a day or two but "for as long as 30 days, renewable by the borrower".

In other words, the Fed became the absolute backer of last resort and through the overnight Fed borrowing window and its bank-only rate -- which the Fed also dramatically cut to make the loans easier to make -- the Fed instantly poured massive liquidity into the market. Poof.

By telling the banking world that it would bail it out short term, no matter what, the Fed once again has acted as the bank of last resort. Throwing out all the noise about creating a moral hazard in so doing, the Fed has a responsibility to make its fiat money acceptable in the marketplace. Period. Of course there was a moral hazard failure. And we're not surprised.

The giant US money center banks once again have learned that they ultimately can count on the Fed to bail them out when they get into trouble. Little banks will go bankrupt or be forced to merge into larger banks (look for this to happen with E-Trade soon). Even big banks may be forced to make their top management fall on their swords. In November, both the Chairmen & CEO's of Merrill,Lynch and CitiCorp -- America's largest investment bank and retail bank, respectively -- were fired. But the banks themselves are going to survive, no matter what.

When Richard Nixon finally yanked the US off the gold standard back on August 15, 1971, there was nothing else left except "the full faith and credit" of the federal government to back up the greenback. So whether the people have confident in their government matters a lot more when it completely controls their money supply in a monopoly-based banking system.

Compare the Fed's actions with that of the poor old Bank of England.

The UK's own sub-prime meltdown occurred this summer when Northern Rock (the UK's equivalent of America's Countrywide Home Loan Bank) had a run on the bank. Consumers heard that Northern Rock's loans were going bad and that their might not be enough money in their coffers to pay back the depositors. Of course this is how modern banking works: borrow short-term and lend long-term. All depositors' money is at risk when most banks today are allowed to lend out upwards of 20 times the money they have on deposit in their 'reserve' account with the central bank. This ain't Switzerland in the 1930's.

But when Northern Rock went to the Bank of England to bail it out with a short-term loan to stem the flow of frightened depositors literally waiting on their door steps, the BofE turned them down. The result was a mini-crisis which morphed into a major crisis and ultimately saw the BofE belatedly pouring over $50 billion into Northern Rock and allowing the damage to spread to the major high street banks like Barclays.

Although the Bank of England is an old hand at issuing and manipulating its fiat currency, the world's master at this game is the Federal Reserve. And the Fed has been able to successfully export its fiat currency (the dollar) and its inflationary policies globally, to the (temporary?) direct benefit of the US consumer.

Meanwhile, it's estimated that the European Central Bank has had to pour over $200 billion into its banking system to bail out the German, French and other Euro-based banks which, strangely, have been investing enormous sums of Euros to buy US sub-prime real estate securitized loans instead of investing in their own home ownership or business development programs.

And on November 26, England's HSBC, one of the top-10 world banks, announced that it was biting the bullet on its own sub-prime portfolio disaster and moving more than $35 billion dollars back onto its own books from funds that it was managing to prevent a forced liquidation at fire sale prices of what it called "high-quality assets". This is probably not a good time to own overseas bank stocks.

Score: Fed 1, World Banks 0. 8 innings -- at least -- to go.

December 3, 2007

EU Fire Sale

JOIN, or DIE.

In Live Free or Die Hard, released in mid-2007, Bruce Willis goes after the bad guys who are sabotaging the US computer systems to steal the assets of the financial markets. In the computer hackers' term, they are creating a "fire sale" that threatens the entire system. Minus the computer hackers, this is akin to what European credit markets are suffering right now.

Alan Greenspan warned us back in 1998 about the real possibility of the world's banking and stock markets locking up and crashing through cascading cross defaults. This problem arises when one bank doesn't have the money to pay another bank which doesn't have the money to pay a third bank and so on.

Originally caused by the burgeoning US sub-prime meltdown, the rot has now begun to spread around the world as bank after bank begins to falter and the international overall system of lending money between banks, the so-called LIBOR facility, has ceased to function. It may cease to exist.

Banks, both inside and outside of the United States, are now terrified of lending unsecured money to other banks – especially the giant banks like Citibank, UBS, Barclays and Deutsche Bank. They're afraid that they won't get repaid, that the bowering bank might default. In other words, mutual trust in the global banking system is now being replaced with fear of uncontrollable bankruptcies. Right now, there is very little "full faith and credit," necessary when you are operating a global Ponzi scheme of fiat money creation.

This phenomena of cascading cross defaults, like falling dominos, is hard to stop once the process begins to roll. It takes massive, really massive, intervention by the central banks to flood the market with cheap dollars, euros, pounds and yen. And the dumping has begun.

On Tuesday, December 11, the day the US Federal Reserve cut interest rates by ¼ percent, the market reacted with confidence by promptly falling 210 points. The was followed the next day by a joint announcement by 5 major central banks (FRB, ECB, Bank of England, Swiss Central Bank and the Bank of Canada) that a coordinated bailout would begin starting on Monday, December 17th.

For its part, the US Fed would pump $40 billion into the troubled US banks through December, followed by perhaps another $40 billion in early January.

The euphoria lasted for one day until the magnitude of the problem began to surface. By Friday, the DOW closed down another178 points. Then the other shoe dropped.

On Tuesday, December 18th, the Bank of England announced that it was effectively nationalizing Northern Rock, the giant failed British saving-and-loan, to the tune of - gasp - $200 billion. Nearly simultaneously, the ECB announced that it would loan its troubled banks - $500 billion – to prevent them from failing.

These numbers are truly staggering.

Never in the history of the world has such a flood of money been dumped into the world's banking system to prop up the banks and get lending going once again. We are in uncharted waters.

The question now being asked by economists, central bankers, stock brokers, finance ministers and heads of state throughout the world is: will this be enough? Or are we in the early stages of the granddaddy of all economic nightmare scenarios publicly envisioned by Alan Greenspan a decade ago? The options look bleak indeed. Either the global money ships make it safely through these iceberg-strewn waters, or the entire convoy is in danger of sinking.

What's this got to do with you, you might perhaps be asking?

Well, if banks can't lend money with confidence, the credit system begins to lock up. Interbank loans -- like the ones banks make to pay off the Visa and Mastercard charges made by the other bank's customers, could be in danger. Your credit card borrowing capacity might be cut -- or stopped. Getting cash from another bank's ATM machine might not be possible. A cash-flow business with lots of receivables like, say, the airline industry, might not be able to continue to fly its planes -- in fear that their bank won't be able to continue making ongoing operating loans at rates they can afford to pay -- so that their suppliers and employees can continue to be paid.

The scenarios are almost infinite and very frightening to contemplate. A global cascading cross default would push the world into a money gridlock. An instant global Depression would result.

Fortunately, calmer minds have estimated that the probability of this actually happening are quite small -- perhaps no more that 10 to 20%. Here's why.

This mess was created by the US in the first instance, and the US can bail the world out.

Over the past several decades the US has been buying lots of cheap goods and oil from China, Japan, Europe and the OPEC countries. And we've been paying for it by issuing mountains of US dollars and shipping them abroad. The balance of trade deficit -- while not terribly large for the US super-economy, the world's largest economy -- has swamped the treasuries of our trading partners.

The foreign central banks have used a number of ways to spend these dollars.

They've bought lots of dollar-denominated commodities (pretty much every commodity traded in the world is traded in dollars), they've bought boatloads of low-paying US Treasury notes, they've bought US land, buildings and companies, and they've bought US stocks and bonds.

Now, it appears, they've also been buying gobs of US sub-prime packaged mortgages.

Once again, the US Wall Street brokers have been successful in selling toxic investments to otherwise smart overseas bankers -- as well as to the US money center banks.

Some could argue that this is the direct result of undoing the Glass-Steagall Act which in 1933 successfully separated banking from investment banking (the stock brokers) for 7 decades. Unfortunately, the stock market abounds in creating new versions of funny money: warrants beget puts and calls and generations of exotic investment vehicles that no one can understand or properly handicap for risk ultimately result in the creation of AAA-bond rated "toxic waste": the so-called CMO's or collateralized mortgage obligations.

But Glass-Steagall is all but dead, killed off in the 1990's by Bill Clinton.

Now that banks can own and operate Wall Street firms, there is no clear firewall to isolate the funny money of the stock market from the funny money of the fiat banking system. The best example of this unholy alliance is the new Citicorp. And, of course, the irony is it may suffer the fate of being broken up into tiny pieces before this debacle runs its course.

So just how does the Fed save the world? By doing two things: 1) providing an unlimited amount of credit to back up the big banks which can't be allowed to fail: Citibank, etc., and 2) by temporarily lowering the reserve requirement that the banks must maintain to conduct business (their shareholder's equity as a percentage of their outstanding loans) down to, say, 3% or so.

The latter could be done by whispering in the ear of the Swiss-based Bank for International Settlement (BIS) which coordinates the world's central banks. So if this round of band aids doesn't work, look for the BIS to announce a lowering of the global banks' reserve requirements in early 2008.

Merry Christmas from the fiat money capital of the world–Washington, D.C. Gold anyone?

December 19, 2007

Moving Deck Chairs on the Titanic

JOIN, or DIE.

So-called Global Warming has the potential to destroy 300 years worth of scientific progress and our advanced western civilization along with it. From an economist's position, it is pure folly. And our worst enemies' dream come true.

Supporters of so-called global warming tend to fall into one (or more) of three categories: politicians who want to use this latest scare tactic as another means to take more control and power over our lives, corrupt businessmen who want to profit by selling snake oil solutions to a gullible public, or ignorant but well-intentioned people who have bought into another fantasy fable.

Al Gore probably personifies all 3.

Certainly his Academy Award-winning Power Point presentation is riddled with flaws. Even high school students have pointed out the numerous factual and apparently-intentional errors. The most important one, of course, completely destroys the basis on which the global warming theory's house of cards is built. Studying his classic temperature versus carbon dioxide chart in detail shows that, on average, atmosphere increases – and decreases -- of it follow temperature changes by an average of 800 years, not the other way around as you are lead to believe.

Causation is not proved just because some event follows another (except among those who flunked history, chemistry AND evolution). However, the inverse does apply. The theory of global warming - namely that co^2 emissions cause temperature increases -- is proven by Al Gore's own charts to be absolutely false. In this case, both temperature changes and changes in atmosphere co^2 levels are likely caused by the same more fundamental event: energy output variations of the sun.

This fact has been pointed out to Al Gore and his believers before -- on numerous occasions. That they have chosen to selectively ignore this scientific fact and have clung onto an increasingly rickety collection of flawed beliefs suggests that they view global warming not as an objective scientific process to be studied and diagnosed but rather a religious experience that transcends rational thought. In other words, Al Gore is a true believer.

Unfortunately, the True Believer is one of the most dangerous and potentially evil persons who can exist. Many decades ago, the San Francisco longshoreman-philosopher Eric Hoffer warned us of the dangers of the True Believer. Karl Marx was a True Believer. Some say that Lenin and Hitler were too. It's hard to tell when a True Believer is also a politician. Sometimes a politician is simply a psychotic megalomaniac who can't envision anyone else being right except himself. Sound familiar?

True Believers are cult followers who when told to drink the poison-laced cool-aid will dutifully obey. The 900 people in Guyana who were mesmerized into following Jim Jones' orders several decades ago killed only themselves. Today's Global Warming True Believers are set to destroy our civilization and economy. Global Warming Kool Aid is no less dangerous than Jim Jones' poisoned brew.

Global Warming is the big elephant in the china shop. It demands all the attention and sucks all the oxygen out of the room.

So really important environmental issues are ignored. Like: 1) dealing with cleaning up the developing world's polluted water supplies which is the number one global cause of disease and death, 2) stopping the destruction of the entire eco-system of the North Sea by giant EU fishing fleets dragging giant metal bars on the seabed scraping away all life in the process, and 3) halting the spread of malaria by using the scientifically-managed application of DDT which -- now that the book Silent Spring by Rachael Carson has been proven to be false -- even the UN says is the right thing to do to stop the needless deaths of millions of people a year in Africa and Asia.

By replacing scientific facts with "consensus" politics, the charlatan can easily manipulate the innocent well-meaning soul. True science, of course, doesn't work on consensus. As Sgt. Joe Friday would say in every "Dragnet" episode, "Just the facts, ma'am". Science is based on provable theories, not emotional feelings.

Moreover, the rational need to make the US into a net energy exporter instead of importer held hostage to OPEC and enemy regimes is also ignored.

Instead of building nuclear power plants to generate clean electricity to power our country -- the way France now does, and pumping our own oil out of our own huge untapped oil fields off our own shores and in Alaska, we continue to whine about the high price of oil and enrich state sponsors of terrorism. We continue to misdirect the government into running up the price of most of the food that we eat - and create global food shortages where there were once surpluses - by redirecting our farmers to grow grains to be made into corrosive and low-energy ethanol to power our cars.

Ethanol is a pollutant perhaps as bad as the previous gasoline additive MTBE -- which was forced upon us in the early '90's by the government to improve the air quality and instead wound up poisoning our ground water in thousands of communities throughout the country. The cure is worse than the supposed problem. Worse, since it has less energy in BTU's then gasoline, mixing ethanol with gasoline lowers the miles per gallon you get in gas mileage. And finally, it costs 50% to 100% more per gallon to produce and to buy. "I'm a politician. I'll save you. Just sign here!"

We're not that credulous. Well, at least not all of us are.

Perhaps, you know someone who, in all innocence, doesn't know the honest facts that support the statement that anthropogenic global warming - as presented - is a lie. In that case, here are a few links to the truth that you can pass along.

First, one of the most incredible reports ever to come out of the US Senate is the U.S. Senate Report: Over 400 Prominent Scientists Disputed Man-Made Global Warming Claims in 2007, released last week by the Senate Committee on the Environment and Public Works. It "lists the scientists by name, country of residence, and academic/institutional affiliation. It also features their own words, biographies, and weblinks to their peer reviewed studies and original source materials as gathered from public statements, various news outlets, and websites in 2007".

Next, the detailed and thoroughly-documented work by Art Robinson, a renowned research scientist, provides step-by-step easy-to-understand analysis of each of the flawed global warming arguments and the data which proves otherwise. After reading this report, all the global warming scales will fall from one's eyes. Complete with 132 footnotes to the underlying source documents in scientific journals and peer-reviewed publications. Enough said.

Finally, Pat Sajak presented 10 questions that he can't seem to get answers to on the subject of alleged man-made global warming. These questions must be answered first.

Global Warming has become the socialist's dream. Create a scary evil monster and then tell the people that only more government regulation of their lives can save them from certain doom. Truly a charlatan's dream come true.

With good science now being published and brave scientists now speaking out against the tyrants against truth, let us hope that 2008 is poised to be a wonderful year in which we can once again return to a world of reason and sanity -- at least in the wacky world of so-called global warming.

* * *

Ronald Reagan: "Progress is not foreordained. The key is freedom – freedom of thought, freedom of information, and freedom of communication."

December 27, 2007

Stark Raving Mad

It took the United States over 100 years to acquire a mountain of silver and another mountain of gold bullion. From the 1790's through the 1920's, these precious metal hordes, stored in Fort Knox and other treasury depositories throughout the United States, were the basis of the wonderful hard-currency American Dollar, that "Little Iron Man" respected throughout the world because it was backed up by these real, very rare and very valuable assets. Those were the days when "as good as Gold" proudly applied to the US dollar.

The Federal Reserve System was created by Act of Congress in the fall of 1913. What had begun as a "good idea" to prevent bank runs of insolvent banks by the Democrats (nearly all the Republicans voted against it) opened Pandora's box of fiat currency and government manipulation of the money supply. As a result, for 95 years, the value of the US dollar has been steadily dropping.

Over the years, the currency was changed too. What was once a Gold Certificate issued by the US Treasury (redeemable at any time for 1 ounce of gold -- often in the form of a US gold coins) became a Silver Certificate redeemable in a sack of silver -- usually silver dollars, half-dollars, quarters or dimes. It was, in effect, a deposit receipt for your real money kept protected in the vaults of the US Treasury.

Then one day, the US Treasury stopped issuing dollar bills, and the control of the US money supply was turned over to the Federal Reserve. Now, the paper dollar bills could no longer be redeemed for anything. They were no longer certificates of deposit; they had become "Federal Reserve Notes", in other words, IOU's by a quasi-government agency. And to enforce the acceptance of these new fiat dollars, Congress legislated that they must be accepted by anyone in business in America. On the US dollar bills, it now says "This Note is Legal Tender for All Debts, Public and Private".

To prevent circulation and hording of real money, the original US gold coins like the $20 Double Eagle were then confiscated by Franklin D. Roosevelt on April 5, 1933, and replaced with $20 paper bills. To refuse to turn in your gold dollars -- or to own gold -- was a criminal offence. The government had taken back the real money from its citizens.

Silver coins like the $1 Liberty or Morgan silver dollar could still be owned, however. To complete the debasement of the remaining coinage, the Treasury had to wait another 30 years.

In April, 1966, the US government ceased to mint silver coins. From then on, all regular US coinage in circulation was made out of cheap base metals. A dollar coin no longer had a dollars worth of silver in it. Instead, it contained perhaps 3 cents worth of common metals.

The transformation was complete. And inflation could begin in earnest, backed by the full faith and credit of the US government, and its 700+ overseas military bases.

For nearly 40 years, this process seemed to work. Each administration could rack up huge deficits which it could wash away by making the dollars it would have to pay back worth less and less in the future. As long as the US was the world's manufacturer a net exporter of products, all was well.

Over time, however, the United States was transformed from an industrial powerhouse into a nation of consumers. It began to farm out its production capabilities, and eventually even its crop growing, to other countries. More and more, the US began to run huge balance-of-payment deficits. Other countries recovering from the ravages of World War II became more productive. Japan and Germany -- our former enemies -- rapidly grew to be the second and third largest economies in the world.

Other countries were receiving shiploads of dollars which they promptly handed back to the Federal Reserve Bank of New York (by now it had taken quasi-ownership of the US Treasury's gold horde) and converted these paper dollars into gold bullion for transfer overseas.

(Well, actually other countries still trusted the US government; they didn't really move their gold out of the United States, they simply had it transferred from the US government's vault in lower Manhattan to their own storage vaults in the same Federal Reserve Bank).

Richard Nixon killed this when he pulled the US off the gold standard on August 15, 1971. By doing so, he reneged on America's promise to pay its debts to the world in real money. Henceforth, US dollar bills and Treasury IOU's would become the world's "legal tender" More and more dollars were shoveled overseas, where they began to float around in their own netherworld of "Eurodollars" and other offshore trading systems. The US FED had become the world's Federal Reserve System. The US benefited mightily. The value of shipping dollars overseas – never to return to the US -- itself boosted the US economy by, some say, as much as 1% of the annual GDP.

And then the European Common Market nee European Community nee European Union began to appear. Charlemagne's European Empire had been reborn. And on January 1, 2002 the Euro materialized to become a real alternative to the US dollar in world commerce.

Fortunately, the US dollar has been so successfully exported it forms the fundamental basis of most of the world's trade and banking. It will be very difficult for the rest of the countries to claw back global monetary control from the Federal Reserve Bank -- to America's temporary benefit.

But the ramifications are clear. Gold is approaching $1000 per ounce. Some economists predict it will reach $5,000 per ounce in 5 years. And the Euro, now at roughly $1.50 is predicted in the extreme to grow to $2.00 to $3.00 as oil is projected to increase to $10 per gallon over the same time frame. Whether these dire predictions come true is yet to be determined.

However, the US Congress is hell bent on helping destroy the last vestiges of the American economic system that has continued to survive -- and has kept the dollar strong(ish).

The best current examples of the US-shooting-itself-in-the-head in the field of economics come under the heading of "reviving the economy". They include:

1) Passing laws to postpone or eliminate the repayment of poor mortgages while at the same time demanding that mortgage companies keep on lending in the future,

2) Dropping the FED's discount (interest) rates with the goal of encouraging more people and companies to get into debt even more,

3) Changing the bankruptcy laws back to more generous terms allowing the debtors to escape their debts -- and driving more lenders into bankruptcy in the process,

4) "Giving" each American family as much as $1200 in cash payments while at the same time loading the new government debt of $1200 -- plus interest payments on it -- on each household in the future,

5)   Banning the incandescent light bulb (which provides some heat in the winter as well as light) and replacing it with toxic mercury and other deadly-substance filled florescent and other new-age lights,

6) Passing laws to force American food production to be diverted to the conversion into energy-inefficient caustic Ethanol thereby driving up the cost of food, and causing more gallons of ethanol-laced gasoline to be burned by drivers, increasing the cost of their daily commuting.

7) Forcing so-called "global warming" laws to make the economy less efficient by spending gobs of wasted money at the government level, by American manufacturers and US households (as compared to China or India which are exempt under the Kyoto Treaty). This to fight a problem which most serious scientists say is not caused by human activity -- and likely doesn't exist in the first instance. (See Dr. Arthur Robinson's recent HUMAN EVENTS article on this subject).

Fortunately, at least two or three of the candidates for President are smarter than this -- and would never allow Congress to do such stupid things. Hmmm... Now which ones were they again...?

*With complements to Art Robinson, Editor, Access to Energy.

"How do you tell a Communist? Well, it's someone who reads Marx and Lenin. And how do you tell an anti-Communist? It's someone who understands Marx and Lenin."
-- Ronald Reagan

For more Reagan quotes, see: The Wit & Wisdom of Ronald Reagan, Regnery Books.

Febraury 6, 2007

Fear and Greed and the Federal Reserve Board

Oh My! When last we looked, the score was Fed 1, Crash 0. That was way back in 2007. A lifetime ago if you're a day-trader.

Greed in the street has now turned into rank fear. And the contrarian investor argues that when everyone is fearful, well that's the perfect time to jump back in to make a killing. So, greed is good. Got that?

In the good old days (say, last October), hope was still blossoming along with the weeds of the sub-prime meltdown mess. Most economists were predicting that the US would squeak through 2008 with slow growth – and just miss going into a recession. The Fed had taken action back on August 17th to allow banks to pony up to the Fed window and hand in sub-prime mortgages at full face value in return for 100% cash in-the-bank Fed money. Several hundred billion dollars in dodgy assets appear to have been handed over to the Fed at the time.

Then, during the week of November 25, 2007, the Federal Reserve Board, acting in coordination with the Bank of England and the European Central Bank (among others), dumped several more hundreds of billions of dollars in liquidity into the marketplace through the creation of new embarrassment-free lending vehicles for the money-center banks (read: Citicorp, et. al.). When all the world's central banks were counted, the total new "loans" provided to the banks exceeded $1 trillion. Now that's beginning to be real money.

Next, on Tuesday, March 11th, the Fed injected another $200 billion into the banking system via weekly auctions where it will lend treasury bills for 28-day periods in return for debt, including "AAA-rated mortgage securities" sold by Fannie Mae and Freddie Mac, and by banks. Loans will be made under a new program called the "Term Securities Lending Facility," to the 20 banks and securities firms that trade directly with the Fed.

This is uncharted water. As Nick Parsons, head of strategy at NAB Capital, said to the UK's Guardian Newspaper: "The Fed is digging a firebreak. The fire was threatening to engulf good assets, bad assets, every sort of asset." It may yet still.

All was calm for another 5 days. Above the surface.

Finally, on Sunday, March 16th, at the start of Easter Holy Week, the Federal Reserve next did the previously unthinkable: it opened up yet another lending "window" at the New York Fed (where do they find the workmen to jackhammer out all these new windows late on a Sunday night?).

This time it was for the major (20 or so) participants in the securitization markets, the New York-based "primary dealers" in things like the US Treasury Notes, to the tune of another (at least) $200 billion. This includes Merrill Lynch, Goldman Sachs -- and Bear Stearns, the 5th largest "investment banker" in the US. Notice that these are stock brokers, not banks. The new window is called the "Primary Dealer Credit Facility."

So, for the first time ever, the Fed has opened its coffers to non-banks. Pundits have asked, "What next, Starbucks and Home Depot?" Perhaps. If it's necessary.

The function of the Federal Reserve System is to keep the money supply stable and the financial monetary system working. Of late, the machinery has been showing a slight tendency to lock up at inopportune times and the Fed's liberal squirts of liquid assets are being made to insure the system continues to be well if not over oiled.

One minor problem did creep up at the same time: the imminent collapse of Bear Stearns, worth over $15 billion on Friday and perhaps a negative $30 billion on Monday morning - if it were forced to file for bankruptcy. The Fed "invited" Bear Stearns and J.P. Morgan, its next-door neighbor in lower Manhattan, to come to an "agreement" whereby JP Morgan would buy Bear Stearns, lock, stock, and new $1.5 billion headquarters building for a piddling $2 per share, or $236 million. As a good will gesture, the Fed threw in a guarantee to JP Morgan to absorb up to $30 billion of doggy assets (more sub-prime mortgages?) owned by Bear Stearns. For its part, J.P. Morgan also set aside a few billion dollars more of its own money just in case.

Finally, to make it worthwhile for the non-banks to turn in their junk collateral to the New York Fed at the new PDCF Window down the street, the Fed dropped its interest rates for the non-banks ¼ point to 3 ¼ %.

When the next regularly-scheduled interest rate board meeting was held on Tuesday, March 18th, Chairman Ben Bernanke and his colleagues further cut the federal funds rate (the interest that banks charge one other) to 2.25 percent, its lowest point since late 2004.

Now we're talking! In response, the stock markets in the US and abroad duly shot up. Although a predictable retrenchment occurred the next day, by the end of Holy Week, the stock markets had recovered, gold had dropped substantially, and even the dollar had firmed up viz-a-viz the Euro and Pound. Holders of Adjustable Rate Mortgages (or ARMS) which are having their rates reset later this year or next can now sigh with relief as they've been given a reprieve of another year or two of cheap interest rates.

Ben Bernanke did his Ph.D. thesis on the Great Depression, and on just what the Fed did wrong in those days - and what the Fed must do in the future to make sure that a great depression will never happen again. Basically, this involves shoveling out of bank windows or helicopter doors potloads of dollars (liquidity) to make sure that we will never have too little money to go around again. Unfortunately, this tactic is also called (at least in the old-fashioned Austrian school of economics) inflation.

The real threat to the system, however, is not the sub-prime toxic waste mortgages being held in the coffers of the investment banks, retirement funds and insurance companies. The Fed can simply buy up all of these if it has to. Jimmy Carter-like inflation of

20% will appear -- but only for a few years at most.

The real threat to the system is the $4-10 trillion (yes, trillion!) dollars worth of CDO's: collateralized debt obligations that the global money system holds. Created as insurance to allow a bond holder to separate the "guaranteed" interest income from the "risky" fluctuating bond selling price, they have seemed to lower these risks until now. The system fails, of course, if the insurer -- the other party to the CDO transaction (like a Bear Stearns) goes belly up. Not to mention that the so-called bond-rating agencies have been rating ZZZ bonds as AAA.

The system itself must not be allowed to lock up. If Bear Stearns went down it would take lots of depositors and cross-transaction parties with it. This could have generated the feared settlement system's doomsday scenario: cascading cross defaults, where, like dominoes, bank A fails knocking down its correspondent bank B which tips over bank C and so on. Along with every person and every business holding assets in those banks.

By its actions over last weekend, the Fed stopped the eminent crash from happening. Hats of to the Fed. Really. Bless you Ben Bernanke.

So, bottom line, the score appears to now be: Fed 2, Crash 1, with lots of innings yet to go. As someone who is perhaps irrationally optimistic, I personally believe that he has an excellent chance of pulling it off. We'll see.

Meanwhile, if you compute the real GDP of the US on a per-capita adjusted basis (divide the GDP by the population), we seem to have drifted into a recession since mid-November. But in GDP-only terms, we're still in positive territory. And a recession, by definition, is 2 quarters (6 months) of continuously falling GDP.

Of course all of this was predicted by Ludwig von Mises. It's what you'd expect when you run a fiat-money system -- and top it up with loads of highly leveraged debt. And we've been doing it for 90+ years now.

March 25, 2008

Obama Tax Policies Penalize,
McCain's Reward

JOIN, or DIE.

McCain versus Obama. In this supposed year of twiddle-dee, twiddle-dumb left-of-center presidential candidates, some pretend it's easy to argue that John McCain's presidency wouldn't be so very much different from Barry Obama's.

Nothing could be further from the truth. When you compare the Republican's tax position of enlightened free-market capitalism versus the Democrat's heavy socialist agenda, the differences become obvious -- especially to anyone who pays taxes. Obama's tax plans will hit the middle class American where it hurts the worst: in his wallet.

Let's take income taxes first.

McCain calls for no changes to today's low rates. Obama will revert to the pre-Bush tax cut regime. Bottom line: if you're single, making $30,000, McCain will tax you $4,500. Obama will extract $8,400 from your wallet -- almost double the take! Single making $50,000: McCain's tax is $12,500; Obama's is $14,000. Single making $75,000: McCain's tax is $18,750. Obama will bite you for $23,250.

And it's no better if you're married. Married making $60,000: McCain's tax is only $9,000. Obama will hit you for $16,000. Married making $75,000: McCain's tax is $18,750, Obama's $21,000. Married making $125,000: McCain's tax is $31,250. Obama's hit -- $38,750. Ouch, Obama!

So much for Obama's plan to tax the "filthy rich". Now we know just what that means: everyone in the middle class.

Well, you say, what about capital gain taxes?

Again, McCain says he'll make no changes. The maximum rate will stay at 15%. Obama is all for change. He'll roll back this tax cut to the pre-Bush rate of 28%, again almost doubling your taxes overnight. This plan is especially cruel to older folks who have planned to sell their bigger homes and count on using this income (after their homeowner's exclusion) to help fund their retirement. Ouch again, Obama.

Then there is the dividend tax.

OK, you've been religiously saving over the decades and buying up blue-chip stocks whose dividends you now count on to carry you through your golden years. Or, you have your savings invested in an IRA or retirement plan, mutual fund or life insurance annuity. McCain's dividend tax won't change from the maximum rate of 15%. Obama will once again repeal the Bush tax cuts, bumping this tax rate up to 39.6%, an increase of -- hold your wallets -- over 160%. The impact on the middle class, much less our barely-growing economy -- are obvious. Really ouch, Obama!

Finally, when you die and have arranged to pass on your hard-earned savings to your family, the differences are truly staggering.

McCain's proposal is, once again, stay the course. His tax rate is zero (Bush repealed the death tax). Obama promises to bring back the bad old days, which will hit the middle class but barely touch his billionaire supporters who've used sophisticated tax planning strategies to escape this tax. Under the Obama plan, the government will take up to 60% of your estate away from your children and family -- and pocket your money via the inheritance tax. For Obama, the politics of envy trumps common sense, fundamental morality and basic economics. So what's new?

Unfortunately, the horror story above is only the start. The Democrats are calling for yet more new punitive taxes on the working and middle classes: 1) a higher federal gasoline excise tax, 2) new taxes on electricity and heating gas, 3) new retirement account taxes, and 4) taxes on "oversized" homes over, say, 2500 square feet are but a few of the wacky ideas being floated.

Of course, if these new taxes actually are passed, the US economy really will tank, and on the Democrat's watch. The economy continues to grow because consumers still have money in their wallets to continue buying -- just. The Democrats would confiscate this money to fund more boondoggle and pork-filled government spending schemes like 3rd-world socialized medicine schemes, so-called global warming carbon credit schemes promoted by Al Gore's profit-making carbon trading company, and ever-expanding government bureaucracy. Who will have any money left to buy that latest plasma TV, much less the $5/gallon gasoline and $10/pound hamburger?

So lots of Americans are dreaming of "change" in this presidential election year. Let's pray that their nightmares don't come true.

One real measure of personal freedom is how much money the government lets you keep to spend for yourself as you see fit. In the old Soviet Union, the communists took almost 100% of the people's earnings in their "worker's paradise". They created a prison state of slaves. It's an old axiom in politics -- and economics -- that the more you tax the people, the more you can control them. McCain's policy is to continue the current relatively low tax program. Obama hopes that he will carry us all into the "Brave New World", a world of draconian taxes that will crush our personal freedoms.

Of course, Obama's words may be all rhetoric and political pandering designed to gain votes. In this case his followers are once again being hoodwinked into believing that his call for "change" is genuine. Let's hope that's the case. This would mean Obama may be cynical -- but rational in his populist strategy. However, suppose he really does believe that what we need is massive tax hikes? May God help us all.

June 17, 2009

HE Exclusive: Interview with Boris Johnson

JOIN, or DIE.

Just 8 weeks ago, on May 2nd, Boris Johnson, the Conservative MP for Henley-on-Thames and former Editor of The Spectator, was elected by a huge 500,000 majority as the new Mayor of London. Overnight, Boris, the blond-haired raconteur and libertarian conservative became Britain's second most powerful politician, holding court over Europe's largest city of 8 million citizens,.

Meanwhile, the Labor Party, headed by the greying Gordon Brown, has crashed in the national polls, and the Tory Party smells blood. The by-election on June 27th to fill Johnson's seat was overwhelmingly claimed by the Conservatives. Labor finished in 6th place, behind the Greens and barely in front of Loony candidate Bananaman Owen, whose slogan was 'Born to be Bananas'.

Meanwhile, Boris, sometimes belittled in the liberal UK press as a 'buffoon', has gone from strength to strength. First, he banned drinking alcohol on the Underground subway cars. Next, he started a campaign to put lots of bobbies -- armed with metal detectors -- on the streets to randomly stop and search 'yobs' suspected of carrying switchblades and other knives. Scores of arrests have resulted.

Then, he announced that, copying his friend Rudy Gulliani's strategy when he was mayor of New York, he would not tolerate 'petty' crime like graffiti. His position -- like Rudy's -- is that civilization is held together at the edges. It's the threads that begin to unwind first. Stop the petty crime and you stop the general rotting proceeding upwards.

Finally, last Thursday, at a first free-for-all US-style town-hall meeting -- unheard of in England - he announced that he would bring back punishment in the schools to improve the abhorrent discipline, and start up a new charity, the Mayor's fund, to enable wealthy citizens and London-based corporations to help contribute to new youth programs to get the hooligans off the streets. His call was met with a roaring cheer from the heavily black and mostly young audience in attendance. Some of the press were shocked.

Human Events caught up with Mayor Johnson (call me Boris) at the Westminster's Methodist Central Hall -- capacity 2,000 -- after his first State of London event. Over drinks we talked about his future plans -- and his advice to the Republican Party in the United States on how to win the upcoming fall elections.

Alexander Boris de Pfeffel Johnson is a very bright and a very witty person. He read Classics at Balliol College, Oxford as a Brackenbury scholar, and was elected President of the Oxford Union, a rare honor. He studied the classics and reads Latin and Greek -- and is seriously proposing re-introducing these languages in London's schools. "I want to encourage more kids from less advantaged backgrounds to top universities -- and that would really help them...and of course education is one issue to do with all the social problems."

Boris also saw the wacky European Union politics up close when he was the Daily Telegraph's European Community correspondent from 1989-1994. In his 2004 successful bid for MP, he's alleged to have said: "if you vote for the Conservatives, your wife will get bigger breasts, and your chances of driving a BMW M3 will increase". Whether it's true or not, it made for a great "Top Gear" quote. Politically correct, he isn't.

But he's dead serious in his politics.

He says he has a simple formula: "we should be free-market, tolerant, broadly libertarian (but not ultra-libertarian), pro-immigrant, anti-regulation, inclined to see the value in tradition, pro-hunting(!), pro-motorist, and pro 'standing on your own two feet'". For a country obsessed with speed cameras, nanny-state politics and big-brother government, these are fighting words. Oh, and he's passionate about riding his bike

And apparently, the British electorate loves every word. Latest polls show that in the next general election, the Conservatives will sweep back into Parliament with a huge majority, sweeping into power with 45.3% versus the Labor's 25.1%.

Boris told Human Events that it's still possible for the Republicans to pull a rabbit out of the hat by sticking to their core values like the ones mentioned above.

"Listen to the people, not the media. Be compassionate but don't continue down the path of ever-bigger government". Boris says he went into politics with a goal: "to cut the government down to size". Having taken over a bloated staff of 3,000 civil-service employees in the Mayor's office, a creation of the former socialist Mayor, "Red Ken", he has work cut out for him.

Having been born in New York City (his family soon returned to England as his mother had yet to take her Oxford finals), Boris described himself as a "one-man melting pot", with Muslims, Jews and Christians in his ancestry. Boris is the great-grandson of Ali Kemal Bey, a liberal Turkish journalist and interior minister in the government of Damat Ferid Pasha, Grand Vizier of the Ottoman Empire, who was murdered during the Turkish War of Independence. So Boris could, some day, become President of the United States.

When we asked him about moving to California to become governor after, say, a respectful 2-term hitch as Mayor of the world's financial city in his preparation for future Presidency, he laughed with a good twinkle in his eye. We suggested that if we couldn't elect the Mayor of New York, than the Mayor of London might be even better. His response: "stranger things have happened". But there's also a chance that he could become Prime Minister in 8 years or so. So the choice for Boris may well become: Prime Minister or President? If he can fix the broken streets and bureaucracy-run-wild London town, he may well take his choice.

July 2, 2008

Oil at $300

JOIN, or DIE.

You would think that this story is right out of science fiction. But the facts appear to be that the US Democrat-controlled Congress intends to destroy the Republican middle class with $11 per gallon gasoline.

The Democrats' base -- wealthy white "limousine liberals", and very poor people -- won't be harmed, but the families who live in suburbia will be devastated.

The multi-millionaires like billionaire Senators John Kerry & Jay Rockefeller, financial speculator George Soros, filmmaker Michael Moore, and actors George Clooney & Meg Ryan can easily pay for their auto and private jet fuel. Poor people are forced to take public transit.

Here's the reasoning behind the move.

The so-called "Global Oil Crisis" is an invention of the US liberal ruling class, which has successfully managed to export their disastrous ideas worldwide. Oil supply and demand has been on knife-edge balance for years. With the growth of the newly well off Chinese and Indian car-consuming populations, oil consumption has been rapidly increasing in the developing world even as it has been dropping in the US. No wonder India and China, with nearly half the world's population, refused to sign on to the Kyoto "global warming" treaty.

Cheap energy -- and specifically oil -- is what made America the powerhouse of the 20th century. When gasoline was $1 a gallon in the US, it was $2-3 a gallon in high-tax Europe. Low US excise taxes enabled the country to grow and our vast middle class to prosper. Even today, the American consumer is paying $4-$5 per gallon of gasoline while his European counterpart is paying $10-12.

To meet this new energy shortfall, economists would assume that the rational market would increase the supply of oil and other oil-substitute energy supplies. But they would be wrong.

First, US the anti-nuclear lobby got the nuclear power industry banned from building new safe and clean fifth-generation power plants, abandoning the field to countries like France, which runs its super-fast trains on nuclear plants scattered throughout the country. In fact, fully 90% of France's electricity comes from 59 non-polluting "carbon neutral" nuclear; they also recycle 99% of the spent fuel into new fuel using a breeder reactor at the La Hague chemical complex. We don't do this either.

Next, the eco-greens got the drilling for new known American oil reserves in the barren wasteland of the Alaska ANWR's near-coast sites, and along the east and west-coasts of the continental US, and in the Gulf of America. Now China & Venezuela are set to start drilling off the coast of Cuba - but not Exxon or Chevron. They're forbidden by law.

Then, the construction of new modern and efficient US-based refineries has been halted for 40 years. So there is a perennial shortage of heating fuel in the winter and gasoline in the summer. One hurricane can take out 5% of the nation's refining capacity for months. A 5% shortfall can now easily cause a $25 price increase.

Meanwhile, the nation's electricity generators, primarily fuelled by coal-burning plants, were forced to convert to natural-gas, previously mostly used in industry, agriculture and home heating. This has, in turn, driven the price of natural gas through the roof, from $3 per thousand cubic feet to over $11.

Finally, the hundreds of older existing oil fields and pumping derricks were closed and not allowed to re-open due to "environmental concerns". California alone has scores of older fields just waiting to be re-opened to increase the US oil supply. And these could be re-opened in a matter of months, not years.

But wait, there's more.

To make matters worse, Congress then mandated using a toxic and polluting chemical -- ethanol -- inefficiently converted from corn, to help alleviate the oil shortage. Corn farmers promptly sold their commodity to the highest bidder, the ethanol refiners. The price of corn-based foods, like cornflakes - and sugar, chicken, milk, eggs and beef has now shot up.

In the process, a minor supply-demand problem has been artificially legislated into a full-blown crisis. The stock market's response has been predictable: down, down, down.

The liberal solution, of course, is for Congress to raise taxes, increase the fuel excise tax, and force industry to adapt wacky "carbon credit" schemes to line the pockets of the rich liberals who are capitalizing on the global warming scare by selling newly-invented credits, like Al Gore's new company is doing. Wrong. This will stress the mostly-Republican middle class even more.

So what is the solution? What's right for America is wrong for the limousine liberals. It's simple, really. Unleash the supply-side forces of economics.

Open up domestic oil drilling immediately. Turn back on the older wells now capped off. Fast-track new safe nuclear power plants. Stop creating global food shortages by killing off corn-based Ethanol production. Waive the punitive duty on cheap Brazilian sugar cane ethanol. Plant lots of domestic switchgrass for cleaner & cheaper ethanol manufacture. Begin a crash construction program of 50 new advanced nuclear power plants nationwide. Stop burning up natural gas to generate electricity. Build new clean coal-burning electric power plants nationwide (China is turning one per week for the next 5 years), and construct coal-to-oil conversion plants. The Germans were doing this in WWII. Alternative-energy sources like cheap 4th-generation solar panels will ramp up as their prices continue to fall.

In other words, return to the old policy of cheap domestic energy that has made America the powerhouse (pun intended) that it once was. The US will become oil-independent of our enemies whose treasuries are now overflowing with a flood of newly-printed dollars we've been using to pay our oil bills with, and the dollar regain its strength as the world's reserve currency.

And the irony? All of this can be done now with results beginning in 90 days, and using new super-clean super-efficient and environmentally-friendly technology. The result: oil will drop down to well below $100 per barrel and the economy will once again boom. If France and China and Brazil can do it, why can't America? Why not indeed?

Oil sells for $145 per barrel mostly because of artificially-created supply-side shortages. A small part of its price is also determined by speculators and uncertainty over a future cut-off of oil from the middle east that a war with Iran could cause. Assuming that Iran's nuclear bomb program is destroyed by Israel this fall -- with or without America's help - look for oil to spike up to $250-300. And 40 years of congressional bumbling will be the cause.

July 4, 2008

Broken China and Other Fragile Structures

JOIN, or DIE.

The miracle of modern economic China has pulled half a billion people from subsistence poverty into a fast-growing market-based economy. These are the blessed citizens who have been able to migrate from the Chinese hard-scrabble interior to the dynamic coastal provinces and super cities. By repudiating the bankrupt economic policies of Marxism, the communist regime has unleashed a tidal wave of entrepreneurial growth, while still keeping a ruthless iron fist to suppress internal political, religious, ethnic and cultural dissent.

From 1980 through 2005, China's average GDP grew by 8.6% per year. This works out to a 786% expansion in the economy, brought about by the replacement of soviet-style collectivist state-owned enterprises with privately-owned and mixed-economy companies. The average wage has risen from under $65 per month to over $6,000 per year.

Nearly all of these benefits have accrued to those fortunate souls who have been able to legally or illegally migrate to the coast from the center of the country. And salaries in Beijing are often many times higher than the average. Hundreds of millionaires and a few billionaires have made their fortunes within the past decade.

However, for the less fortunate billion people still trapped as serfs working under the old corrupt state-owned farming and factory system, life is brutal and people still scrape by on subsistence wages.

Which parallel-world China you live in, Coastal China I or Interior China II makes all the difference. Lately, the serfs of the command-economy China II have begun to grumble. And there are a lot of them.

The central government has been inflating the money supply faster than its real growth rate. By pegging the Yuan at an artificially low exchange rate of 7 Yuan to the US dollar, over a trillion dollars (one thousand billion dollars) has wound up in the state bank's coffers as Americans are enticed to buy intentionally-underpriced products from the Chinese. In effect, China's policies are subsidizing the American consumer, who benefits from a higher standard of living than would otherwise be possible. But such a policy is unsustainable in the long run -- for both countries.

This 18th century producer mercantilist strategy to grow through cheap global exports has created enormous economic structural problems as hot money continues to pour into China. Boom after boom is followed by rounds of ever-growing busts. The stock market advances 100% in a year and then crashes back 50% in a few months. Real estate overbuilding is endemic in China I.

China's money supply has now been growing by double-digits for a number of years. And inflation is having a severe impact on the vast hinterland. Rice has doubled and tripled in cost, and the poor interior can't afford to pay the going market price. Food rationing of rice and other staples has begun in China II, soon to be followed by increased starvation, food riots and a crackdown by the army. The conventional socialist solution, likely to be applied -- massive state subsidies and price controls -- will only serve to prolong the agony and continue the shortages.

In the meanwhile, back on the coast in China I, China has been preparing for a global P.R. exercise, the 2008 August Olympics show-and-tell.

Once the last foreign visitor departs, the Central Bank will be forced to finally revalue the Yuan upwards. How much so is the 64 billion dollar question. Some analysts estimate that the Yuan is undervalued vis-a-vis the US dollar by as much as 60%. But even a 20% upward revaluation would wreck havoc with its economy.

If the Chinese-made plasma TVs, children's toys and household items suddenly become more expensive for the western consumer, their demand will drop and substitutes from Indonesia, Thailand and Malaysia will appear to take over the market share. The result: closing factories and massive layoffs in the tens or hundreds of millions of workers and a serious economic crisis for China's ruling elite.

The resulting reduction in domestic consumer purchasing power will drive down the demand for certain commodity imports including steel and aluminum. A global fall in many commodity prices will likely result as a knock-on effect.

The Chinese ruling clique is sitting on a running tiger. If the tiger suddenly brakes, they will be thrown off -- and in danger of being eaten. One solution to this dilemma is to rapidly reposition the economy from primarily export-driven to domestic consumption.

Developing the infrastructure, rebuilding the creaking state railway system, and providing new modern power systems is necessary but not sufficient.

China is already building massive coal-fired electric power plants at the rate of one a week (so much for fighting so-called 'global warming'). Within a decade, China is predicted to out-pollute the US and Europe combined. And Beijing is already a toxic city of massive factory and car pollution.

For the Olympics, the central government has ordered factories in Beijing and the 5 surrounding provinces, including Shanxi, to close for two months from late July to try and clean up the air so that western tourists will actually be able to see blue skies. Many residents of Beijing are being "encouraged" to visit relatives in distant cities so as to cut down on automobile pollution and lower the congestion. The sight of thousands of Olympiads wearing face masks (as much of the ordinary population now does) beamed to the billions of viewers worldwide would not help promote the Chinese self-image of a world power.

China needs to create a massive middle class of consumers,

and fast, to enable its factories to continue to employ the legions of new workers migrating from China II and to transition away from the failed 18th Century mercantilist model to the truly free-market model as advocated by Adam Smith.

Whether it can do so in time remains to be seen -- for the half-billion people who live in coastal China I as well as their billion poor cousins living in inland China II. Its success, or failure, will impact the world's economy greatly and to a lesser degree the US economy as well.

June 28, 2008

Lazear Talks Fannie, Freddie, and Change for 2009

Ed Lazear is the Chairman of the President's Council of Economic Advisors (CEA). He is a Professor of Economics and Senior Fellow at the Hoover Institution (Stanford University), now on leave.

He is one of the White House's key decision makers involved in last week's take-over by the Federal Government of the Federal Home Loan Mortgage Corporation (FHLMC) (NYSE: FRE), popularly known as Freddy Mac, and The Federal National Mortgage Association (FNMA) (NYSE: FNM), commonly known as Fannie Mae.

These colossal publicly-traded mortgage companies have together lent over $5 billion to Americans to enable them to buy and own their own houses. Every other American's home is financed by these two behemoths. And they are in deep trouble.

HUMAN EVENTS met with Mr. Lazear in Tokyo several days ago for a private interview after he presented his professional views on improving the U.S. health care system to the Mont Pelerin Society, the global organization of Noble-Prize-Winning Economists and other distinguished professors and free-enterprise think-tank leaders.

Ed began by talking about the current mortgage debacle and housing crisis. "The bailout was a done deal a year ago. But we were still shocked when we finally got to take a look at their books. Freddy Mac was a dark hole. It was much worse than we thought when we saw their numbers."

He revealed that Freddy and Fannie "had moved away from their core business of making classic home loans and had entered the hedge fund business in search of higher profits. At one time they even owned oil futures!"

Fannie Mae was created in 1938 as a government agency under FDR's "New Deal" to provide liquidity to the mortgage market. Until 1970, Fannie Mae held a virtual monopoly on the secondary mortgage market in the United States when Freddy Mac, also created by Act of Congress, entered the marketplace.

On September 7, 2008, James Lockhart, director of the Federal Housing Finance Agency (FHFA), announced that Fannie Mae and Freddie Mac were being placed into conservatorship of the FHFA, the most sweeping government intervention in private financial markets since the Great Depression.

Lazear noted that "clearly, the independent regulator of these two firms was unable to catch the problem itself". There was no alternative but to exercise the Federal Government's right to place the two into conservatorship if the taxpayer's money was going to be used to bail out the businesses. Under conservatorship, we can control the future of the organizations and conduct a rapid reorganization and bring in expert new management."

Lazear told HUMAN EVENTS that "it also reduces some of the moral hazard. Old management is now gone, and the common shareholders are not being bailed out. Their equity has been wiped out anyway. The stock prices are down 90% since January".

The "bailout" will take the form of guaranteed loans by the Treasury at 10% interest, and so he expects the government to actually make a profit on its investment as the real estate market recovers. The numbers are substantial, however. Analysts estimate that upwards of $100 billion each may be needed. Still, this is a fraction of the portfolio of home loan assets that the two institutions own and small compared with the roughly $600 billion that China and Tokyo have spent in buying Freddy Mac and Fanny Mae bonds.

Lazear also observed that "the Fed is also now re-examining

the rules on lending in the housing market". When it was observed that much, if not most, of this problem of making dodgy loans was the result of Congress "encouraging" banks to make "no doc, no equity" loans, especially to poorly-qualified minority buyers in the late 90's, he tactfully declined to comment.

Lazear expects the housing financial market to begin to recover in 2009. But his views on the global economic slowdown are not as clear. "Many people, particularly in Europe, thought that the rest of the world had become 'decoupled' from the U.S. market. People forget that international trade now accounts for over 25% of U.S. GDP, up from only 10-12% a few decades ago. A slowdown in growth or other financial change in the US economy can have a far greater impact in other countries."

Turning to the subject of inflation in the United States, Lazear thinks that "this has been principally caused by structural impacts, not monetary policy. The effects of high energy prices, including oil and natural gas, have rippled through the economy affecting most prices."

He states that "the main problem on the inflation front is not loose money, but high energy costs."

Moreover, "the overbuilding of houses has been a relatively recent growing phenomena. Low interest rates encouraged the annual construction of 2 to 2.1 million housing starts, an excessive supply compared with a demand of 1.5-1.8 million units, just a few years ago."

Coming back to inflation, he stated that "the core figures are up a little but some others are now dropping." He noted that "oil is the overwhelming driver of upward prices. The growth in oil consumption from 2000 through 2004 was fairly modest. Since 2004, the demand has actually been dropping, and that is having a dramatic effect in falling oil prices, per barrel."

However, he observes that unless we increase domestic oil production dramatically, "even if we brought monetary inflation down to zero, we will still see crude oil prices fixed at current high prices."

He clearly does not accept the argument that some members of Congress have argued -- that the price of oil has been driven up by speculators. When it was observed that if a speculator is in the market, it takes a willing producer on the other side to do the deal, he agreed: "[S]peculators in the oil market, taking a position against the oil companies, generally lose just as much as they make, but they represent a tiny fraction of overall oil trades."

As the world absorbs the ongoing shock of the U.S. financial liquidity problem, now being played out in Wall Street, the effects of the clearly coupled U.S-global markets is expected to have an ongoing ripple effect from market to market and country to country. In the past few days alone we've witnessed the collapse of Lehman Brothers, the merger of Merrill Lynch into the Bank of America and the AIG debacle. Let's hope that Chairman Lazear is right in his predictions of a recovering financial system in 2009.

September 17, 2008

Clinton-Appointed Raines Has Ties to Fannie Mae, Obama

JOIN, or DIE.

Now that the Obama attack ads are falsely accusing the Bush Administration and the Republicans of causing the current financial crisis, it's important to set the record straight over exactly how this dodgy home loan program -- and its run-on domino toppling of the nation's biggest banks and investment banks -- began. And, yes, it's once again the Democrats' fault. Surprised?

The story is, as usual, one of government manipulation of the free-market.

Before President Clinton and the Democrats in Congress intervened, the home mortgage business was healthy and stable, and housing prices were gradually rising in tune with the overall market (driven, of course, by the gradual increase in the money supply by the Federal Reserve, otherwise known as "monetary inflation").

Here's what happened.

On November 12, 1999, President Clinton repealed the Glass-Steagall Act, which for 55 years had prevented banks, the nation's lenders, to get into the so-called "investment banking" business (stock brokers). With lots of pressure in Congress by the Democratic members of the New York contingent, the Senate and House caved in and trashed a law which had provided stability in both the banking industry and on Wall Street.

What follows next reads like a third-rate screen play.

Banks jumped into the fray, and, encouraged by the Wall Street Democrats, began buying up and merging with Investment Banks, swapping assets, creating new loan "instruments" and weakening both independent systems.

Also in 1999, Clinton appointed Franklin Delano Raines, a Harvard Law School graduate and his Director of the U.S. Office of Management and Budget (OMB), to become the CEO of the obscure but powerful Fannie Mae giant GSE (Government Sponsored Enterprise), which had been "privatized" and listed on the New York Stock Exchange.

Mr. Raines immediately went to work lobbying Congress for less regulation and more "flexibility" in creating the massive dodgy-loan portfolio of under-qualified home loans to fellow minorities which would continue to grow and was encouraged by Barney Frank, another former Democrat & Harvard Law School graduate who now heads up the House Financial Services Committee -- which has key oversight over both Fannie Mae and Freddy Mac.

The good results of Mr. Raines' efforts soon became apparent.

On December 21, 2004, Raines accepted what he described as "early retirement" from his position as Fannie Mae's CEO while U.S. Securities and Exchange Commission investigators continued to investigate alleged accounting irregularities. The Office of Federal Housing Enterprise Oversight (OFHEO), the regulating body of Fannie Mae, has now accused him of abetting widespread accounting errors, which included the shifting of losses so senior executives, such as himself, could earn large bonuses.

Then, in 2006, the OFHEO filed suit against Raines in order to recover the $50 million in personal payments made to Raines based on Fannie Mae's overstated earnings which were initially stated to be $9 billion but have since been reduced to under $6.3 billion.

Undeterred, Mr. Raines now works for another Harvard Law School graduate, Mr. Barack Obama's presidential election campaign -- as an advisor on mortgage and housing policy matters.

Meanwhile, continuing pressure by the New York Democratic Congressional caucus encouraged both retail banks and the new mortgage subsidiaries of investment banks to also make home loans to less qualified borrowers (read: low income, poor-credit, deadbeat, and undocumented liars) -- if they wanted to continue to be able to benefit from light supervision and aggressive merger and acquisition practices.

By the end of the '90s, no less than nine separate, independent, and uncoordinated Federal Regulators had been created by Congress. These agencies included the SEC, CRTC, Controller of the Currency, Treasury, FRB and OFHEO, among others. They would poorly supervise what Clinton had now given birth to: a jungle of speculators, favor-seeking financial lobbyists, and Democrat-dominated Wall Street organizations who duly poured millions of dollars of contributions into Democrat coffers for the Congressional and Presidential elections.

By the time that "Securitization" of home loans (Fannie Mae began to convert its original business of making mortgages to creating packages of home loans that it could sell off as safe investments on Wall Street) began to grow, the Democrat Senators and Representatives cheered the wonders of the new-found ability of America's financial community to enable the poorest and least-qualified of their voters to finally be able to own their own homes.

U.S. home ownership, averaging around 65% for 50 years, suddenly jumped up to almost 70% -- and the housing construction sector took that cue to start building even more houses on spec, knowing that they would soon be bought using doggy loans.

Fixed rate mortgages gave way, under encouragement by the legislators, to so-called variable-rate ARMS and low-initial-entry-cost loans ("sharks").

In 1998, Senator Chuck Schumer of New York was elected. He now serves on both the Finance, and the Banking, Housing & Urban Affairs Committees, and is the Chairman of the powerful Housing, Transportation and Community Development Subcommittee. He also graduated from Harvard Law School.

After the sub-prime mortgage industry began its meltdown in March 2007, Schumer proposed a bailout by the Federal Government of sub-prime borrowers -- ostensively to prevent these poor-credit owners from losing their homes. Financial commentators immediately observed that such a "bailout" would primarily benefit Wall Street bankers and other lenders -- who had made large campaign contributions to congressmen. (Schumer's nine biggest campaign donors are financial institutions -- who had contributed over $2.5 million to his re-election campaign.)

As the recent Indy-Bank collapse occurred, CNBC financial analyst Jerry Bowyer said that "Schumer was responsible for the second largest bank failure in US history."

The final invention of the new-world-order of funny money was the "Credit Default Swap", a derivative instrument which resembles an insurance policy but, in fact, can be used to magnify raw speculation profits -- and down side risks -- and was, ahem, generously exempt from regulation or even transparency.

The conditions had been set for a gigantic credit collapse and subsequent financial world meltdown which is continuing as we write. All from a simple idea to "help the little people" -- who would show their appreciation by re-electing the Democrat politicians who were the vocal cheerleaders (and recipients of gobs of doggy-lender re-election campaign funds).

So the pattern becomes clear. Harvard Law School attorneys -- noted for their lack of economic knowledge -- create an easy-money system which relies on flakey loans provided by fat-cat financial manipulators who are the primary contributors to the re-election campaigns of the legislators -- almost exclusively Democrats.

But this makes sense.

Demographers have shown that since the 1940s, the Democratic Party has segued from the party of the working middle class to the party who's voters look like a double-hump camel: they are either the poor who vote for entitlements or the extremely wealthy millionaires and billionaires who provide the "juice" to buy the allegiance of the first group.

Meanwhile, the Republicans have morphed from the fat-cats (who are all mostly Democrats now -- see the Obama campaign donation records at www.fec.gov) to the party of the working and middle class which saw landslide support for an ex-union-leader and Democrat-turned-Republican, Ronald Reagan.

The solution is simple: the Democratic Party in control of the Senate and House needs to get back to its roots and stop being co-opted by the world's wealthiest -- and financially manipulative -- Wall Street "titans".

A return to the values of the small business owner would be a good start: hard work and personal savings, not get-rich-quick (like the Democrat-voting dot.com billionaires). Small business is the real growth engine of the American economy, and these "mom and pop" shops employ the majority of our citizens.

This may be more difficult than it seems, however. Small business owners strongly empathize with people like Gov. Sarah Palin and her fishing-boat husband, not Joe Biden, another attorney who turned professional politician one year out of law school, in 1969.

So what's next?

The U.S. Government will create a Resolution Trust Company to temporarily take over the perhaps $1 trillion doggy-loan portfolios of the nation's lenders and free up the grid-locked system to start inter-bank lending again so the free-market economy can continue to grow. This "New RTC" will eventually dispose of its portfolio -- hopefully, as before, at a profit for the taxpayer.

A centralized regulator, most likely the Federal Reserve, will subsume most of the other eight regulators. Regulations which worked for decades, like Glass-Steagall, the up-tic sell rule and sound-accounting regulations may be restored.

And maybe, Congress will remove its addiction to the Wall Street money re-election game. Without the latter, of course, we can expect to see another, worse, financial fiasco in the next decade or two.

Since our fiat dollar currency is now only backed by the "faith and credit" of the United States" (there isn't any politician-proof gold or silver backstopping this fiscal house-of-cards, Kennedy & Nixon killed them off), it's inevitable. We'll see.

September 22, 2008

Watching the House Burn Down: What Caused Our Economic Crisis?

JOIN, or DIE.

What caused our economic crisis? The housing bubble caused it.

What caused the housing bubble? Sub-prime mortgages, risky mortgages, to low-income, bad-credit borrowers.

Where did they come from? The "Community Reinvestment Act" (Google it. Read its Wikipedia entry).

President Jimmy Carter and the Democrats passed it in back in 1977. It gave incentives to help low-income borrowers get a home.

Not a bad idea - if done right.

It helped a little, but only a little -- until 1995.

The Clinton Administration and the Democrats in power added massive new provisions to authorize -- require -- sub-prime loans be made. The revisions went further, by allowing the securitization of CRA loans containing sub-prime mortgages.

That forced banks to issue $1 trillion in new "sub-prime" Loans.

The CRA requires that deposit-taking financial institutions (read: banks) offer equal access to lending investment and services to all those in an institution's geographic assessment area -- at least three to five miles from each branch. Before the CRA, many bankers excluded low-income neighborhoods and people from their lending products, investments and financial services -- a practice known as "redlining".

Community activists coined the term when they discovered that the failure of banks to make loans to some low-income neighborhoods was so geographically distinct, that it was easy to draw red lines on maps to delineate the practices.

Of course, marketers have recognized for years that the United States is a nation of multiple communities each with its own distinct education,income, and religious, social, cultural and consumer values and beliefs. You can check out your own zip-code for free using the PRIZM system (See: www.claritas.com/MyBest-Segments/Default.jsp?ID=20).

By 2000, the CRA was funneling millions, perhaps billions of dollars to left-wing "community activist" groups. The Clinton Administration had turned the Community Reinvestment Act into a Democrat piggy-bank and "a scheme against the nation's banks".

And created sub-prime mortgage securities.

Bear Sterns was the first company to do it. Remember them?

Fannie Mae added fuel to the fire by purchasing $2 billion of dodgy "MyCommunityMortgage" loans.

And sub-prime mortgages started to grow. Between 1995 and 1999, Fannie Mae Sub-prime Alt-A & Other Purchases grew from under $2 billion to over $16 billion per year!

Now home prices started to rise - from under 2% to over 6% per year, year-after-year.

Fannie Mae is a "Government Sponsored Enterprise". Fannie Mae guarantees mortgages and then Fannie Mae sells them to banks and investors. The more mortgages, the more money Fannie Mae makes.

So how do you increase the number of mortgages? You move down the 'income ladder' (see: Washingtonpost.com: Fannie's Perilous Pursuit of Sub-Prime Loans).

With "affordable mortgages", fixed-rate loans were replaced by variable-rate loans (ARMS) and in turn by interest-only loans. These new loans gave "flexibility to lenders by allowing variances that borrowers need to qualify for loans". (CSRwire). These variances applied to: loan-to-value ratio, borrower contribution, housing expense-to-income ratio, among others. In other words, to flakes.

Remember, the banks had to issue sub-prime loans or pay big penalties to the government.

How do you keep these loans "affordable"?

No money! No money down! Interest only! Low variable rate! No income verification! Bad Credit! No credit! No problem! Just sign here! ("Moneyfor nothing -- and the chicks are free!").

By 2004, 92% of Fannie Mae's sub-prime loans were variable rate.

Fannie Mae told the banks "Make the loans -- we'll guarantee them".

Home ownership kept rising -- and so did prices, and the demand for houses rose too.

But demand for loans caused the interest rate to rise. Basic supply and demand 101 stuff. High-school students are taught this. Apparently not Senators or Representatives.

Then, gas prices shot up. Paychecks got squeezed. Especially low-income paychecks. Some borrowers stopped paying -- so banks stopped lending. New ARMS and other "affordability loans" dropped from nearly 20% of total market share in 2006 to just 10% in 2007.

So the sub-prime market collapsed. From Fourth Quarter 2006 to Fourth Quarter 2007, Sub-prime mortgage originations dropped from $140 billion to under $18 billion, a drop of 88%.

Foreclosures started pilling up. No buyers, only sellers.

Home prices started falling. Down 2%, 4%, 6%, 8%...

More borrowers stopped paying. 60 day+ delinquencies went from under 8% in 2006 to over 25% by mid-2007.

Fannie Mae "Guarantees" became worthless - because they kept overstating their assets. (See Bloomberg.com: Regulators Spin Public to Boost Fannie, Freddie).

Banks collapsed due to worthlessness. Government Sponsored Securities issued by Fannie Mae became worthless. Jobs disappeared -- and here we are. (See Guardian.co.uk: 'IMF says US crisis is largest financial shock since Great Depression').

Why is the expansion of the Government's Community Reinvestment Act to blame?

Before CRA expansion, home prices simply increased with the underlying inflation rate, going up by 200% from 1975 through 1995 as the dollar dropped in value by the same amount. Home prices and home ownership rates were essentially flat - after adjusting for inflation. After CRA, home prices became unhinged from inflation, jumping 100% from 1996 to 2006 while inflation increased by 'only' 33%.

CRA caused home prices to rise too fast. Economic fundamentals did not support this growth. Government regulation-mandated credit did.

A bubble -- waiting to burst!

So, did it have to happen?

NO!

The Bush administration and some of the members of Congress (read: John McCain) proposed to create a new agency to oversee Freddie Mac and Fannie Mae (See NYT: Sept 11, 2003). "The Bush Administration today recommended the most significant regulatory overhaul in the housing finance industry since the savings and load crisis a decade ago". "A new agency would be created within the Treasury Department to assume supervision of Fannie Mae and Freddy Mac."

But the Democrats in Congress stopped it: "Supporters of the companies said efforts to regulate the lenders tightly under those agencies might 'diminish their ability to finance loans for lower-income families'". Barney Frank said everything was just fine: "The more people exaggerate these problems, the more pressure there is on these companies, the less we will see in terms of 'affordable housing'".

This, of course, was wacky. By now, the creation of dodgy loans created a demand for housing -- which drove up the price of all houses -- and pushed the price of housing out of reach for the very people the CRA was supposed to help. And by 2007, the home ownership rate was falling - rapidly.

The time bomb was ticking.

John McCain's "Housing Enterprise Regulatory Act of 2005" was neatly shot down by his Democrat opponents (See: www.govtrack.us Bill S-190).

Fannie Mae had friends in the Senate: Senator Chris Dodd (D-CT) and, the new junior senator from Illinois, Barack Obama, who proceeded to appoint Jim Johnson, former head of Countrywide Mortgage, and Lehman Brothers, and - Fannie Mae - as his close personal advisor. (Johnson was also Democrat Walter Mondale's campaign manager for the 1984 presidential race).

He's now on the board of Goldman Sachs (which used to be run by our current Secretary of the Treasury, Democrat Hank Paulson). See: Center for Responsible Politics (www.opensecrets.org). Golly, it gets incestuous.

Nobody likes discrimination. Everybody deserves a home. Not a house of cards.

Poor people didn't cause this debacle. Free markets didn't cause this mess. Deregulation didn't cause it.

A bad federal law caused it - that forced main street banks to become predatory lenders to fulfill a well-meaning but economically-bankrupt government mandate to offer souped-up, shell game "affordable mortgages".

Self-interested lawyers continued the fiasco, along with greed and stupidity on Wall Street (and fear of powerful politicians in Congress).

So what were created were lots of "affordable mortgages" that people couldn't afford - and the rest of us will get poorer in the process.

Bad social engineering caused this mess, creating the environment and the wrong incentives that set up low income families to fail, to have their dreams torn away by reality while getting Wall Street to finance it all - and drive itself into bankruptcy in the process.

This is what you get when you let idiots and socialists run the public policy of the United States Government - especially our fiscally-bankrupt fiscal and financial policy.

A lot of the above ideas - and the wording - were taken directly from researchers at John McCain's election campaign. You can't improve on the perfect. It's amazing they got it so right. (See: www.youtube.com/watch?v=H5tZc8oH--o).

But will any of these facts make any difference?

September 29, 2008

The Global Depression of 2010 Awaits

In the good old days of 2005, the US dollar's share of the world's financial system had dropped to around 60%. The dollar was slowly losing its status as the global reserve currency as the Eurozone became a reality and the Euro began to be held in reserve in the central bank coffers of Japan, China, Brazil, Russia, India, the UK, and others.

Then the October crash of 2008 happened, and the world suddenly became aware of the profound lurking global systemic risk to both its financial system -- and the real-world's global trade. It turns out that the world was really much more interconnected than ever before, and the fantasy of "uncoupling" from the United States and its financial system was just that -- a fantasy.

For over 400 years, Letters of Credit have financed the world of international trade. An importer's bank, say CitiCorp in New York, extends a letter of credit through the exporter's bank, say HSBC in Hong Kong, to guarantee that the exporter will be paid when the shipment of goods arrives at the dock in New Jersey. Or the trade could run the other way, when a mid-west farmer plans to ship wheat to an importer in west Africa.

When the US credit crisis arose, banks worldwide immediately stopped lending to each other, since they couldn't be sure that their correspondent bank would be around in a month or two to pay back the loan. Worse, so-called cross-default provisions between the major banks make the risks of lending to an unsure partner even worse. Trust among the banks collapsed. Even trust between operating subsidiaries of the same bank overseas were strained.

The result?

Banks stopped extending letters of credit to finance global -- and even some domestic -- trade.

Unfortunately, most bulk cargoes and global commodities as well as finished goods are financed in dollars -- as are their commodities futures contracts written in Chicago, New York and London.

When US banks stopped extending loans to overseas banks, overnight there appeared a profound shortage of dollars available for non-US banks to continue their international trade. And unlike the US -- where the international export-import sector accounts for only 25% of the GDP- in dollars (and most of that is inside the NAFTA zone between the US and Canada and Mexico) -- many other countries count on foreign trade to provide from 50% to 70% of their economies. Even France & Germany, while inside the Eurozone, depend upon cross-border trade for 60% or more of their GDP.

The world's desperate demand for dollars soared. Most companies doing business internationally buy and sell based on dollars.

Today, the US dollar's share of the world's finance -- the so-called "reserves" -- has probably shot up to over 65% -- and is perhaps above 70% and growing. Who knows?

No one wants yen, rubles, renminbi, pesos, pounds or Swiss francs. Even Euros are worth less outside the closed continental Eurozone. The dollar has gone through the roof. BNP-Paribas predicts that the Euro will again drop below the dollar in value and UK analysts predict a similar fate for the English pound by early 2009.

But still global credit is in short supply. And without import-export credit, global trade grinds to a halt.

Consequently, the Baltic Dry Index -- used to measure the cost of chartering bulk cargo vessels for goods like corn and wheat, iron ore, cotton, rice and other "dry goods" -- has collapsed by over 90% in 2008.

When wheat can't be shipped, the distant country's mills can't turn it into flour. Bakeries can't bake bread. Stores can't sell bread. Shortages occur. People are laid off. They stop spending. And no one can pay their bills when they are laid off or their firms go bankrupt. A recession turns into a global depression -- caused by cascading real-world defaults caused by the banking system lock-up.

Meanwhile, back in the US, important trading nations like Canada, Mexico, Brazil, and South Korea continue to be favored by the Federal Reserve with directly injected liquidity (money). China and Japan are OK too -- they have their own hoards of US dollars -- as do Saudi Arabia and the Gulf oil countries. They are firmly inside the US dollar zone. Likewise, the 12 European Eurozone countries controlled by the European Central Bank (and indirectly the UK) are also able to maintain most bloc trade independent of the dollar.

As the world begins to unwind, people stop buying things. Sales of imported wine and toys and clothes drop, along with purchases of imported and domestic-made cars. GM and Ford totter on the verge of bankruptcy, dragged down by their bloated domestic union contracts which suck up all the profits made by their booming overseas divisions. Now their overseas divisions are slowing down too. Even mighty Toyota is crashing.

Worse, no cash is available -- especially from the terrified banks -- to build new modern plants and assembly lines. Planning on buying a clean all-electric car soon? Forget it. Ditto clean nuclear power plants or wind farms. Like the old days of Soviet central planning, the entire system is quickly being starved of investment credit.

Then the government politicians and bureaucrats step in to "save" the banks and then the automobile companies and then the credit card companies and then the next industry sector to fail.

Bailouts await Intel, Apple, and HP as the entire system becomes morally corrupted. Even Walmart will be too big to fail...

What the politicians are really doing with all these so-called bailouts, of course, is trying to save their own skins, afraid of an angry populace which will wake up in time for the 2010 general election and toss the present bunch of rascals out of Congress.

By then, US unemployment will have reached 12% and your 401K plan will be renamed the 101K plan (except for members of the auto workers union whose own retirement plans will be bailed out by taxpayers money in exchange for their votes).

Eventually, when the whole sorry mess crashes down around us, people will remember warnings that so many of the founding fathers made in cautioning against creating a central bank. The Fed will be replaced or dissolved, and a new free-market system will emerge like a Phoenix without a corrupt politicized and easily-manipulated fiat currency to rot it out from within.

Sorry Mr. Obama. You inherited this mess, and the only solution to save our collective skins is a big dose of Austrian free-market capitalism, not a soul-crushing dollop of state-administered socialism. You must let the incompetent, the corrupt and the foolish fail.

A recession is like a brush fire which quickly burns itself out as it clears the dead wood.

But heavy-dose money-printing management of the economy, starting with the Fed and Treasury's morally-bankrupt programs is about to turn a short and severe recession into a catastrophic forest-destroying monster depression.

If you, Barack Obama, have the audacity to turn 180 degrees to embrace this reality, you will probably be remembered in the history books as the greatest-ever president who saved America -- and the world.

On the other hand, if you stick to a "progressive" wealth-destroying socialist-Marxist big-government agenda, we will be cursed to suffer for decades.

So one can hope.

The other sad option takes us down the road to the solution that finally got us out of the 1929 Great Depression: the second world war. God help us if that is the route we take.

November 19, 2008

A Story of Christmas Past, and Christmas Future?

Courtesy of Dr. John Rossi, as shared with Glenn Beck

Every once in a while, a very special story comes along to remind us how blessed we've been in our Republic -- and how threatened it is as we rack up bills totaling trillions of dollars in IOUs and the spectre of massive inflation, socialism and the systematic destruction of personal freedoms continues to grow like a cancer in America.

Glenn Beck read this on his radio program on December 8th. It was written by Dr. John Rossi, who handed it to Glenn while he was making his book tour rounds in Florida earlier this month. Here it is:

"Once upon a time there was a very happy couple. Their names were Freedom and Capitalism.

They married and had many wonderful children. Their names were Independence, Self-worth, Hard-work, Dignity, Charity, Faith and Hope. They all lived happily for many years and the children respected their parents and loved them both very much.

But Freedom and Capitalism later had several naughty children, very naughty. They weren't so respectful and never appreciated their parents.

Their names were Wealth-envy, Environmentalism, Animal-rights Activism, Racism, Feminism, and Ultra-liberalism.

These evil children blamed their parents for everything and hated their parents Freedom and Capitalism. In fact, these unappreciative children began to hate their parents, since they didn't realize their parents gave them everything they had and didn't realize that they wouldn't even exist without their parents.

They hated their parents so much that they began to plot with their neighbors to kill their parents and to keep their home.

Their neighbors' names were Socialism and Communism, whoon the outside were a very lovely couple, but inside they were very, very ugly.

They and their children, whose names were Despair, Poverty, Suffering, and Repression had been welcomed into every neighborhood they had lived in. Eventually, they were thrown out of each neighborhood after years of suffering and the loss of many lives.

So late one night in total darkness -- because Socialism and Communism did everything in darkness and away from the light of the truth -- while everyone was asleep, Wealth-envy, Environmentalism, Feminism, Animal-rights, and their younger obnoxious brother, Hollywood, disguised Socialism and Communism from recognition and let them into the house of Freedom and Capitalism.

It wasn't hard to sneak in, for the two parents, Freedom and Capitalism, always left their gate and their door open for everyone.

Wealth-envy led the way because he knew the house oh, so well. The evil children then led Socialism and Communism throughout the house, one room at a time.

And one at a time they killed Hard-work, then Dignity, then Independence, Self-worth, Charity and Faith.

They finally found the room of Freedom and Capitalism and killed them as well. It wasn't hard to do, since Freedom and Capitalism always left their door unlocked and open for everyone.

Only Hope survived. Hope survived hiding in the closet. She ran out during the ensuing celebration.

After Socialism and Communism moved in, things went well for a while, but then they decided they didn't like Freedom and Capitalism's evil children, either. They wanted their own children to have the rooms in their new house.

So late one night in total darkness -- because Socialism and Communism did everything in darkness and away from the light of the truth -- they sent their children to kill Freedom and Capitalism's remaining evil children.

Poverty and Suffering killed Environmentalism and Animal-rights first, for they were so hungry, they had to kill all the animals for food and the trees for their wood. And besides, why should animals have rights if people don't?

Hopelessness killed Liberalism, the retarded brother of Communism. Then Poverty, Suffering, and Repression killed Feminism, the retarded sister of Liberalism.

And Hollywood, the young obnoxious son of Freedom and Capitalism, was also killed.

Finally, Wealth-envy, who had originally led the attack on his parents, died at the hands of Poverty since there was nothing left to envy.

So Socialism and Communism and their children, Poverty, Despair, Hopelessness, Suffering, Repression lived in the once beautiful home of Freedom and Capitalism which was now in great disrepair and they all lived sadly ever after.

All that was left of the family of Freedom and Capitalism was Hope, who was quietly hiding in the woods."

Dr. John Rossi lives in Florida and hopes to turn his piece into an illustrated children's story one day and is looking for an artist and a publisher to help. I hope he finds both -- and soon. Little Hope needs to be able to read something to keep up her faith out there all alone in the cold and dark woods as she reads this Christmas Story (of the future?)

December 25, 2008

Human Events Quizzes Bernanke at London School of Economics

JOIN, or DIE.

Federal Reserve Chairman Ben Bernanke flew into London to meet with Governor Mervyn King, his counterpart at the Bank of England, and Prime Minister Gordon Brown at #10 Downing Street on Tuesday. He then went on to deliver the annual Joseph Charles Stamp Memorial Lecture entitled "The Crisis and the Policy Response" to our current global financial system meltdown.

Human Events was there to cover the event -- and to quiz Dr. Bernanke in the Q&A session on his Keynesian approach to the systemic money problem. The world's media covered the event live, including the BBC, CNBC, Fox News, CNN, and Bloomberg. For a clip of our Q&A, see: CNBC Video.

OK. So here's the problem. Keynesian solutions just don't work. Throwing money from helicopters (or more likely C-17's today) might just pull us out of the Great Depression II, but as we stretch the rubber band, eventually the block of deadweight banking system credit will finally spring to life and violently overshoot way before future Fed and Treasury Secretaries can reel in the excess money.

The result? Massive inflation from 2010 onwards. 25-30% would not be surprising through the teens.

Yikes! (That's a techno-speak economist term for holy s***, it's that bad...)

So if you think gold is high at $850 today, wait until it reaches $3,000 a troy ounce. Ditto commodities (especially agriculture).

Jim Rogers has been warning about this probability for the

past year. He's been riding the commodity prices all the way down in the process -- and he's still positive about their future. I, for one, wouldn't easily bet against the co-founder (along with George Soros) of the Quantum Fund.

At the London School of Economics, former home (1931-1950) of Austrian-school founder and Nobel Prize winner Fredrich von Hayek, Dr. Bernanke went on to point out all the Keynesian goodies he has in his "toolkit" which the Fed is using to overcome the crisis.

Chairman Bernanke acknowledges that the bottom line problem -- which began with the funny-money mortgages politically made to underqualified borrowers -- has seqway'd into a full-blown global loss of trust by just about everyone, consumers and bankers alike, in the present financial system. Or, in FedSpeak: "Rising credit risks and intense risk aversion have pushed credit spreads to unprecedented levels…Heightened systemic risks, falling asset values and tightening credit have in turn taken a heavy toll on business and consumer confidence and participated a sharp slowing in global economic activity. The damage, in terms of lost output, lost jobs, and lost wealth, is already substantial".

Of course, the unspoken statement is that the reason that the people don't trust the present fractional banking system -- and are hording their precious cash -- is that the entire system is a house of cards, or more like the game of chairs where the last person standing when the music stops doesn't have a chair to sit on. And nobody wants to be that last person standing when the music stops.

Bernanke goes on to observe, chillingly: "the global economy will recover, but the timing and strength of the recovery are highly uncertain". That's telling it like it is.

The Fed's toolkit -- which has been newly invented over the past 18 months -- has three groups. They "all make use of the asset side of the Federal Reserve's balance sheet". This means, they consist of creating more money out of thin air.

"The first set of tools, which are closely tied to the central bank's traditional role as the lender of last resort, involve the provision of short-term liquidity". It's important to note that the reason the central bank is known as the "lender of last resort" is that when it collapses, the entire edifice falls and a new system must be built to replace the old.

In these cases, the political system often falls as well. Whether a free-market-oriented democracy or a socialist-oriented totalitarian system springs up to replace the former ruin depends on the people -- both the average citizen and the elite.

The question is, what kind of new system will arise from the Federal Reserve ashes? Another Keynesian Ponzi-scheme or a solid hard-money-based Austrian-school bank? The reason, of course, that Austrians like gold is it can't easily be counterfeited by the government. It's quite a "barbaric metal". In the people's hands, it can't easily be controlled by the bureaucrats. Darn.

It may just be possible, however, that Bernanke and colleagues can begin to move the Federal Reserve away from a fiat-based money system. You don't really think there's money in the banks to cover all your deposits, do you? And what do you mean by money, anyway: "legal tender IOU notes"?

Bernanke knows this all too well. And if he can get us through this Keynesian-induced hell with just one more dose of Keynesian money printing, then maybe he'll have the time somewhere in the future to move the system back to a gold-standard dollar. Hmmm...

The tools in the first set are: 1) cutting fed funds and "discount window" interest rates, 2) increasing the length of the overnight "discount window" from 24 hours to 90 days, 3) the new "Term Auction Facility" which lends more money to the banks for "good" assets, 4) the new "Term Securities Lending Facility" which allows certain stock brokers to borrow money from the Fed for "less-liquid collateral", and 5) the "Primary Dealer Credit Facility", yet another bail-out loan facility for otherwise bankrupt stock brokers.

In addition to the above "short term" loan programs to US banks and stock brokers, the Fed has printed up more US dollars to convert into foreign currency using "bilateral currency swap agreements with 14 foreign central banks". Why? Because the world has run out of dollars to spend in paying its bills! No problem, we'll print up some more dollars for you too. Happy to oblige!

The second set of policy tools "involve the provision of liquidity directly to borrowers and investors in key credit markets". They are: 1) money printed up to purchase commercial paper, 2) money printed up to purchase money-market funds, and 3) a Fed-Treasury joint money printing program to buy up AAA-rated student loans, auto loans, credit card loans, and SBA loans.

Finally, the third set of new "policy tools" includes creating more money to buy up longer-term securities including $600 billion in Government-Sponsored Enterprises (GSE's like Freddie Mac and Fannie Mae) and GSE-backed securities. The home mortgage market "dropped significantly on the announcement of this program". The message: don't bet against the Fed's ability to print mountains of dollars -- at least in the short term.

The result of all this newly-created money is that the Fed's own balance sheet -- which took 90 years to reach the first $800 billion -- is now well on the way to $3 trillion, and that's all money created out of thin air.

Consequently over the next 6 months, look for the Fed to bail out ever more failing financial institutions -- starting with another multi-billion-dollar kick to the near-bankrupt Bank of America. This second round of funny money will be followed by a third and perhaps more, until we'll all be swimming in a sea of dollar bills. As the recession bites deeper, the velocity of money -- how fast we spend it -- slows precipitously, and huge doses of more raw money are perceived by the money controllers as the only way to pull us out of this government-created mess.

What else can they do? The Austrian economist Murray Rothbard revealed the simple answer in his History of Money and Banking. Politicians everywhere need to read it immediately.

Professor Bernanke is a genuinely likeable person with a good sense of humor and a deep knowledge of how the financial world really works. He was warmly received by the LSE students and faculty in London.

Unfortunately, he is also the head of the biggest fiat-banking scheme ever devised by mankind. And he knows it. (Thank you John Pierpont Morgan for your Jekyll Island creation.)

The tell is that his voice waivers when he is saying something that he hopes will come true but is unsure of. Listen to his speeches yourself and you'll hear what I mean immediately. It's the giveaway of a basically honest and decent man. Bernanke still needs to fully master the "FedSpeak" of his predecessor, Alan Greenspan.

Alan could easily tell the House Banking Committee about how the Fed was fully in control - and there was nothing to worry about. And they believed it. Yet he was a protégé of Ayn Rand and the author of a marvellous essay on the need for gold-backed central banking in his youth. Years before he too became the head of the Fed.

I truly hope that Chairman Bernanke can pull it all off just one more time. Like a junky hooked on ever-increasing doses of the good stuff, I need just a little more money, please. The withdrawal is too painful and I don't want to hurt that much. I promise to go straight and reform in the future. Trust me. In fact, trust all of us. We're all in this together.

January 16, 2009

Cap and Trade: A New Disaster Waiting to Happen in 2009

Heard of so-called "global warming"? It's been shown to be another socialist scam to create massive government controls over a "crisis" which doesn't exist. But, as Rom Emanuel, President Obama's closest advisor has said, good socialists "never let a serious crisis go to waste." Especially if its imaginary.

Want the facts on global warming? Almost 900 scientists and experts from dozens of countries recently met for the 2009 International Conference on Climate Change in New York. Their consensus -- based on reams of detailed surface and satellite-orbiting sensors, and ice core samples, is that the earth is actually cooling, and it's caused by the sun's unexplainable recent reduction in output energy. See: Heartland for dozens of papers, keynote addresses, videos, PDF's and data results.

No problem. "Cap and Trade" is not really about so-called global warming. It's really designed to secretly extract $2 trillion per year in hidden "consumption taxes" to pay for the bloated pork, earmarks, "stimulus" and "bailout" programs that the US government has recently created to pay off their Wall Street cronies and lobbyists.

Here is what the US version of "Cap and Trade" is all about:

It's a program which will apply a tax on all release into the atmosphere of carbon (in the form of carbon dioxide) that a person generates, beginning with you personally exhaling. Never mind the fact that carbon dioxide is a trace gas which accounts for 0.0385% (you got that right, it's 385 parts per million) of the atmosphere, and is a plant food! Never mind that carbon dioxide in the atmosphere can't increase much beyond it's present level given the fact that above a certain level, the atmosphere cannot chemically absorb any more CO_2 and the rest falls back onto the surface of the earth to be absorbed by the oceans or by new plant growth (more food) and tree cover (more forests). Never mind the fact that the world's forest and plant coverage is up by over 20% the past few decades (fewer people to starve and to build wood houses). Never mind that carbon dioxide increase in levels trails by 750 years behind the warming of the earth. (They re-ran the ice core data using newer more accurate and detailed analysis techniques. Opps, there goes another of Al Gore's false global-warming slides out the window).

The new "Cap and Trade" tax - at the federal level - is actually a "consumption tax" on:

1) your breathing (no joke!) - an estimated charge based on the average person's body weight and added to annual income tax.

2) physical things that you purchase (all involve the release of carbon) including: clothes, books, magazines, computers, automobiles, DVD's, medicines, etc. To be applied to the manufacturers of these items who will then pass along the additional carbon taxes to the consumer (you) as an increase in the selling price of the product. Since all manufacturers and importers will be affected, the tax will be passed along by all of them as across-the-board price increases. Be sure to add this new tax on top of the increase in liquor and cigarette taxes now being implemented. And while we're at it, be sure to tax the tax by adding state sales taxes on top of your total purchases. If you're a socialist government, taxes are good. Right?

3) Food products that you eat. To be applied to the farmers of all food items who will then pass along the additional carbon taxes to the consumers as increased food prices. Meat products such as beef and pork, chicken, milk, cheese, butter and yogurt will be taxed at a much higher rate than low-carbon-consuming foods such as tofu, spinach, lima beans, etc.

4) Services that you consume. To be applied to all suppliers of services such as cinemas, newspapers, TV & radio stations, telephone, cable, satellite and internet companies, database providers, restaurants, fast-food outlets, dry cleaners, real estate agents, airlines, travel agencies, hotels, gardeners, doctors, attorneys, accountants, water and trash companies, local and state -- and federal -- government agencies. These hidden taxes will be passed along to the end consumer as increased charges in services and fees.

5) Energy that you consume. To be applied to all energy supplies that you consume. Honesty will prevail here. This will be listed as a direct tax on your bill. Includes: gasoline, natural gas, heating oil, electricity consumed by you personally or by machinery that you operate or businesses that you own or control. Look for gasoline to jump back above $3-4 per gallon -- or more.

Estimated costs: In excess of $2 trillion/year to be paid for by 300 million American consumers. That's roughly $6,600 for every American - including babies, and older people in retirement homes. Or, for the 50% of households who actually still pay taxes, that's about $38,000 in new taxes per year. Creation of a new federal government mega-agency requiring 50,000 new government employees with enforcement and arrest powers will be required, along with 350 new government offices with surveillance capability. This new super agency will be needed to manage the new "excess energy consumption" supertax and it's denial-of-access powers for the piggish home consumers.

For example, the installation - as currently mandated by some states -- of new electronic controls of all residential electrical meters with remote control by the power companies and the State Energy Government grid agency will be able to remotely monitor your personal electricity consumption on a minute-by-minute basis and charge rates accordingly. Look for the new federal law to require all power companies throughout the United States to plug in their newly-installed home monitors to a massive new Washington, DC-based consumer and business "Federal Emergency Power Control Center".

Excessive consumption (as defined by the bureaucrats) will be supertaxed or alternatively your house electricity controller which will replace the electric meter can be instructed to remotely turn off the entire house power or kill the power to selected devices such as air conditioners, electric heaters, lighting, pumps, etc.

The automobile industry will be instructed to install mandatory GPS systems in all newly manufactured cars to supplement the "black box" monitor which has already been hidden under the driver's seat for the past 15 years. This box currently records up to 48 hours of car data - accessible by the police when an accident occurs - to store speed, breaking, direction, acceleration and other vital data as a person drives, including (in some models) interior audio conversations. Did you know your own car already has one of these?

The new GPS system will enable the Federal Government to real-time track all vehicles at all times, and to compute "excessive traveling" by "chronic travelers" and directly bill the registered vehicle owner via a new federal surtax on his annual state DMV car renewal tax.

Expect this bill to be introduced in Congress this year. It's being pushed by President Obama who last week stated it was his highest priority to pass such legislation before the end of 2009.

This bill is a simple massive tax increase (mostly hidden), buried in purchase costs of items you consume. This false legislation will become law because the Federal Government is near bankrupt and needs this new tax - introduced under the guise of "protecting the global environment" - to pay it's bills.

Note that the calculated so-called "benefit" in the reduction of carbon dioxide (there goes the food supply) created by the reduction in consumption that this tax will "encourage" when fully implemented - will be made completely worthless by just 6 months of increased Chinese growth in energy consumption during the year 2009 alone.

The Chinese are now building 2 new dirty coal-fired electric power plants per week, and are now producing over 1 million automobiles per month - while the US sales of our ultra-clean automobiles has collapsed to roughly 800,000 per month.

Economists estimate that the introduction of President Obama's "Cap and Trade" law will increase the US unemployment rate by 1% -1.5%. Estimates for people out of work in the USA for 2010 will rise to over 12%, and growing.

My personal estimate is that we could see unemployment rise to between 15% to 20% (Depression-era figures) by 2011 caused by all the massive bone-headed socialist spendthrift legislation now being introduced by the Federal Government, this legislation included. Cap-and-Trade is the true socialist's dream as it addresses a non-existent problem with a massive series of new hidden taxes and a massive increase in federal government bureaucrats and police with monitoring and control powers to use against the citizens of the United States.

Of course, "I'm just saying", as Glenn Beck likes to say "I could be wrong". Maybe "Cap and Trade" won't pass a responsible Democrat-dominated Congress in 2009. Hmmm.

April 14, 2009

How Socialism Works in the Real World

JOIN, or DIE.

David Kamerschen is a professor of Economics at the University of Georgia who has fun teaching economics to new students fresh to the field. Lots of people who teach economics, including yours truly, have used a variation of David's illustration over the years. It never fails to hit the mark -- if not Marx.

Econ 101 or its equivalent is usually a required course for most college students, most of whom groan when they are forced to take a class in the "dismal science". That's because they never were exposed to real-world lessons in economics when they were in grade school. If we begin to teach our children the facts about how things really work when they are 8 instead of 18, we'd get much smarter voters at 18 -- and far less mushy-thinking socialist "progressives".

Bar Stool Economics:

Let's suppose that a group of 10 graduate students regularly go out to a pub for beer, and the tab for the 10 comes to $100 total. If they pay for their bill the way Americans pay for our taxes (based on our so-called "progressive" tax system), the breakout would be like this:

The first 4 people (the poorest) pay nothing. They get to drink for free.
The fifth pays $1
The sixth pays $3
The seventh pays $7
The eighth pays $12
The ninth pays $18
The tenth person (the richest) pays $59.

Being good friends and liberal progressives, that's what they all agree to do. It seems only fair that each person should pay what they can afford to pay, remembering the old adage they learned in school: "from each according to his ability, to each according to his need" (Karl Marx).

Every few days, the 10 good friends would meet up in the pub and would pay up as agreed upon.

Then one day, the proprietor gave them a deal. "Since you are such good customers, from now on", he said, "I'm going to reduce the cost of your tab by $20. You can just pay me $80!"

Everyone wanted to continue to pay their bill just the same way as they had before. So the first four people (the poorest) are unaffected. They continue to get to drink for free.

But what about the remaining 6 people? How should they split up the unexpected $20 savings "windfall" so that everyone would get "his fair share"? They figured that $20 shared by 6 comes out to $3.33 each. But if they simply subtracted that amount from each of the 6 paying friends, then person #5 and person #6 would actually be paid to have their beers since person #5 only paid $1 anyway and person #6 only paid $3!

What to do?

The pub owner came to their rescue. He suggested that each person's bill should be reduced by roughly the same amount, and he used his calculator to work out what that should be:

Persons 1-4 continue to get to drink for free
The fifth person, like the first four, now pays nothing and drinks for free (100% savings!)
The sixth pays just $2 instead of the original $3 (33% savings!)
The seventh pays just $5 instead of the original $7 (28% savings!)
The eighth pays just $9 instead of the original $12 (25% savings!)

The ninth pays just $15 instead of the original $18 (17% savings!)

The tenth pays just $49 instead of the original $59 (16% savings!)

All 6 friends were better off then before. And their first four buddies continued to drink for free, because they didn't have a lot of money.

They all felt pretty good about it.

After they thanked the pub owner and left to walk back to campus, they began to compare their savings under this new deal.

The sixth person was very quiet, though. Finally he blurted out. "You know, splitting up the bill that way wasn't fair! I only got a dollar out of that $20 we all saved, and yet (he pointed to the tenth person) he got $10!"

"Hey, you're right", shouted the seventh person. "I got cheated too. I only saved 2 dollars. It's unfair that he got back 5 times more than me!"

"Damn it! I've been ripped off too", yelled the eighth. "Why should he get back $10 when I got back only $3. The wealthy get all the breaks!"

"Wait a minute", screamed friends one through four. "We didn't get anything at all! The system exploits the poor!"

The first nine people surrounded the tenth person and beat him up.

The next day, tempers had cooled down and the nine friends showed back up at the pub. They were sorry for what they had done and they wanted to apologize to their tenth friend.

But the tenth person didn't show up for drinks. So the nine proceeded to drink without him.

When it came time to pay the tab, they discovered that they had a problem. They didn't have enough money among all nine of them to pay for even half of the bill!

"And that, boys and girls, journalists and college professors, is how our tax system works", says Professor Kamershen. "The people who pay the highest taxes get the most benefit from a tax reduction. Tax them too much, attack them for being wealthy, and they just may not show up anymore. In fact, they might start drinking overseas where the atmosphere is somewhat friendlier."

President Obama and the Democratically-controlled congress, good wannabe socialists all, should remember this lesson before all of the rich people (mostly Democrats, by the way, but that's the topic of another article) stop going to the pub with all their other good friends. Raising taxes using a "progressive" tax system penalizes the productive, wealthiest members of our society much more than the average taxpayer. And I'm against that even though it would hurt the many Democrat billionaires far more.

And once we tip over the edge where 50% of the population don't pay income tax at all (the first five "good friends"), we create an us-and-them mentality where the first five vote in the politicians they want to continue to get their beers for free.

But there's no such thing as a free lunch. Someone always pays. Until they can't or don't anymore.

John Galt couldn't have said it plainer.

May 14, 2009

Interview with Future Prediction Expert Gerald Celente

JOIN, or DIE.

It's the end of the world as the Greater Depression hits after 2010's failed "W-recovery"

Human Events had the opportunity to interview forecaster extraordinaire Gerald Celente, President of Trends Research Institute, several days ago -- and the future he predicts looks bleak indeed. In fact, as Mr. Celente sees it, the Great Depression will seem like a mild recession as what waits for us in 2011 hits with the force of a Katrina financial hurricane.

In case you're wondering who Mr. Celente is (if this is still possible), he's appeared -- along with his predictions -- on Oprah, CNBC, Reuters, NBC, PBS, BBC, the Glenn Beck Show -- the list goes on an on. His Trends Report has been successfully predicting the major future trends impacting our lives for 3 decades, including calling the dot com crash back in the 1990's.

Mr. Celente's forecast on our impending future is based on his study of history. He says we are bent on destroying our currency, bankrupting our government, and unleashing a violent citizen-against-citizen eruption as the economy collapses into chaos and martial law fascism.

Quite a claim. And God help us if he is right -- again.

"We're sounding the alarm about the ongoing downward economic cycle", Gerald told Human Events. "In 2002, we predicted that the collapse of the American empire would fall like the World Trade Center in a thunderous crash -- in slow motion before our eyes. And now it's happening."

Mr. Celente follows over 300 trends: family, crime, war, education, consumer & business patterns which TRI synthesizes to predict the future.

"The US is becoming a shadow of what it used to be. Take education for example. The OECD group of developed countries ranks quality of life, education, health care of its member nations. The US is now falling down the table as one piece of data after another shows America is in decline. We're no longer Win, Place or Show in quality of life, education, longevity... all the essentials where we used to be #1. And our economic underpinnings are failing."

Mr. Celente puts part of the blame squarely on the federal government, and especially FED Chairman Bernanke and Treasury Secretary Geithner, and warns us not to believe a word they say "They're the same people who didn't see it coming - are now telling us the worst is over, that 'green shoots are spouting upwards'. But they were wrong before. They're wrong on this too".

"When you pump out tons of money manure into this system based on nothing – printing press paper, it's like giving a patient with a chronic disease a pain killer -- it won't cure the patient."

"But let's go beyond the economics. Our whole Constitution has been abrogated. The president simply writes an Executive Order to do whatever he wants. Nationalize the banks, take over the insurance industry, automobile industry, health care industry... None of it is constitutional."

When did the problem begin?

"After Dwight Eisenhower -- our last great president -- the Allied Supreme Commander in WWII – who warned us of the dangers of the military-industrial complex. We've become completely corrupted."

"We became enmeshed in foreign entanglements. We forgot the lesson of England - and how their global imperial overreach destroyed their empire."

Of course, the average American doesn't think that we're an empire. We're not like the classical empires of old - raping, pillaging and stealing the wealth of invaded peoples. What does Mr. Celente have to say about this?

"What we're doing is squandering our wealth, our resources, the genius of our scientists and the future of our children. We're over-consuming in every way -- but under consuming our education and focusing on the quantity, not the quality, of what we've built. So much of today's culture is counter-productive to what American built it's foundation on -- a high-quality producing nation building things, not pushing paper.

"And we've become not only a consumer society but a low-quality consumer, as well as the most obese society in the world, eating low-quality high-carb, high-fat processed foods."

"We're now focused on the lowest cost, the lowest common denominator. Not the best and highest quality. We advertise buying cheapest as the most important thing."

Mr. Celente argues that we've socially destroyed our productivity and have abandoned it to other countries.

"And we have fallen into a moral vacuum. Look at how people used to dress. Smartly. Not like the cheap hoods of today. Fashion now copies the lowest common denominator. Our children wear clothes without belts, and shoes without shoelaces, to copy the styles of the violent criminals -- who have these items removed by the police in prison so they can't be used as weapons. That's become the fashion statement of today's youth. Like rap music from the ghetto. We've become an underdeveloped nation."

Mr. Celente observes that "people used to think of America as that shining beacon on the hill with 'liberty and justice for all...'." So what happened?

"Morality is missing from our American public consciousness. Start with Wall Street. It's run by a criminal gang. The only question is 'how much can you make, how much can you steal?' At the bottom, the welfare recipient says 'how much can I take?' And the government is in on the take."

"Morality is absolutely the issue. We had a government where we were taught all our lives that we are a free enterprise system -- so we depend on our own strength, our entrepreneurial ideas. The world used to look to us for our innovative spirit."

"This is being destroyed before our eyes. And our government has become more interventionist than any of the old empires could imagine."

"Our society is now based on consumption -- 70% of the GDP. This is more than we produce. So to pay our bills, we use funny money invented in 1913 with the creation of the Federal Reserve and the fiat dollar based on credit (debt) -- the fractional reserve system. In 1930's you bought what you could afford. You saved up to buy your home. The easy credit of the 90's has destroyed the country. Now you borrow what you can't afford - and the nation's done the same."

Mr. Celente predicts the use of printing press money will cause the "greater depression".

"I predict continuing deflation of real estate, followed by extreme currency inflation -- ultimately becoming worthless. This is why gold is the only honest money -- the government can't counterfeit it. Look for it to top at least $2000 an ounce"

"Our unemployment numbers are also bogus. For example, the construction industry is really above 20% , and the government is creating low-level jobs, not real jobs. The US total real unemployment is more like 16%. Before the crisis is over, it will reach 25% - great depression numbers."

"When people have lost everything they have nothing to lose. Violence and crime will explode. Look at the OECD figures. The number of people not graduating from high school is exploding -- they're wacked out on drugs. New York City will look like Mexico City in a few years. The collapse of morality from top down -- and especially in the government -- makes it inevitable."

"What can we expect in the coming future", we asked.

"Washington has declared 'Economic Martial Law'. Wall Street is putting Main Street out of business. The key to watch is Christmas sales. They'll fail. Christmas will be when reality sets in."

"Another trend we wrote about over 2 years ago was the tax revolt. What's happened? Tax revenues have collapsed by 33%. And the wealthy people are leaving."

"We predict state secessionist movements will rival the breakup of the Soviet Union."

"The only way we can ever recover is to return to individual community, personal responsibility, local government. Next, average will disappear, Quality will return. Look at GM. Junk cars financed by junk bonds. Now owned by a junk government. As a consumer, don't consume quantity -- consume quality."

"How will it all end?", we queried. Will the dollar survive?

"The dot com bubble should have burst and gone away in a short sharp recession. But the boys at the Fed re-inflated the economy by lowering interest rates to a 46 year low -- and in turn created the real estate bubble -- much bigger than the dot com bubble. "

"Now they're creating the bailout bubble -- which will ultimately dwarf the real estate bubble. It will cause the implosion of the global economy world wide -- which will not be able to be repaired by creating yet another bubble. Every time the government fails, it tells a bigger lie and then a still bigger lie."

"These previous bubbles were not allowed to pop -- but they

didn't destroy the infrastructure of the country. This bailout bubble will."

"But this bubble will be the last one. After the final blowout of the bailout bubble, we are concerned that the government will take the nation into war. This is a historical precedent that's been done over and over again."

"So, it's not that the dollar that will survive. We may not even survive. Look at the German mess after WWI. It gave rise to Fascism and WWII. The next war will be fought with weapons of mass destruction."

American 'Liberal Fascism' ?   Is it possible?   Jonah Goldberg's bestseller raised the alarm two years ago.

June 5, 2009

US Economy's Future is Controlled by 3 Companies, and They're Not Goldman Sachs, JP Morgan or CitiCorp

JOIN, or DIE.

If the United States were Japan back in the 1998, its credit rating would too have been downgraded by now from its AAA credit risk to AA+ or lower. Indeed, the once-stellar credit ratings of European countries Ireland, Italy, and Spain have already been shown the axe. Spain's unemployment is now edging upward towards 20%.

Ireland's recent loss of its coveted 'Triple-A' status has touched off a financial crisis which is rapidly deteriorating into a political crisis. As a result, the center-left party will probably be swept away and replaced with a pro-business center-right party when the voters next get their chance. As the say in Europe, "we like to vote in the socialists when we're feeling fat and full of cash, but when times get tough economically, we like to replace them with the 'grown ups' who won't run our country into the ground fiscally".

The UK is also teetering on the brink of losing its cherished AAA status. And with it will go the pound (down) and unemployment (up).

How does the credit worthiness of a country affect its fiscal health? And why should the politicians and bureaucrats in the White House, the Treasury and the Fed be quaking in their boots right now?

Simple.

If a country, like the US, should lose its pristine credit rating, it will instantly lose the ability to sell its bonds to many potential buyers. And, God knows, with all the monster deficits being wrung up by the White House these days, the US government needs all the newly minted Treasury Bills – in the tens of billions of dollars - to be safely sold, without fail, week after week.

The fate of the US government hangs in the balance by the analysts at the three global credit rating agencies who daily measure the financial health of 125 countries. They're akin to the 3 personal credit bureaus whose "Fico scores" compiled by the Fair Isaacs company determine whether you can get a credit card or car loan or even a decent home mortgage.

With a really good Fico score, like 800 or above, you'll be offered the lowest loan interest rates. As you score drops down to the 700's and 600's, your credit risk goes up, and borrowers begin to disappear. Those that remain will charge higher interest to make the same loan. Your risk of defaulting on the loan jumps. Drop below 600, and you probably can't get a loan from anyone except, perhaps, the local loan shark – at 10% interest – per month.

Unfortunately, many major buyers of bonds -- government or corporate, US or overseas – have restrictions on what they can legally buy. US Treasury bonds are often owned by central banks of other countries -- like China -- and retirement programs, mutual funds and pension funds. Many are only allowed to own only ultra-safe 'Triple-A' rated 'paper'.

Lose that rating, and the next day, the market will see hundreds of billions of dollars of US government Treasury bonds dumped as 'secondary sales' -- perhaps at fire sale prices.. When such an oversupply of sellers dumps T-bills, their price will fall smartly, and the Treasury bond interest rates will skyrocket, as many of the potential buyers are forced to sell too. So the cost of borrowing money both short and long term will spike up. Then, almost immediately afterwards, the interest rates on credit cards, corporate borrowing, and most importantly, home mortgages will shoot up as well.

The rating agencies are terrified to tell the truth. Because the US is the principal money center on the planet, and because the US dollar is the world's reserve currency, such a lowering of the US AAA rating -- which it has maintained for over a century -- will ripple through the global economy as bond and stock markets recoils in shock and follow the US downward. Credit rating agency fees will soon follow.

They have not yet downgraded the UK pound-based 'Gilts' (government bonds). These are on the ropes as the UK has been faithfully following in the US footsteps by taking over its banks, printing up funny money to pay the bills, and running massive government deficits to add its own 'stimulus' package to the economy. Naturally, the UK's unemployment rate is shooting upwards as well.

The UK's Labour (socialist) government is teetering on collapse with the lowest voter rating in over 100 years. The fall of their government, due to the fiscal incompetence of Prime Minister Gordon Brown, the former "wunderkind" Chancellor (their equivalent to the Treasury Secretary) and his decade long spend-and-spend policy, is predicted to occur this autumn, if not sooner. When that happens, the dam will likely break, and the UK will be stripped of its AAA rating.

The pressure will immediately shift to the US as overseas money -- now funding 50% of government bond sales -- begins to flee. Interest rates will go up as the Treasury must continue to conduct ever-bigger weekly bond sales to fewer and fewer buyers. Eventually, the other show will drop, and the US will lose its Triple-A rating as well.

This is uncharted territory. Over the past few decades. countries like Mexico, Argentina, and Zimbabwe have seen their ratings plummet -- along with their standard of living. Unemployment figures have recently reached 25% or more in other developed countries. But not yet in the US.

Faced with the problem of declining bond sales and raising

interest rates killing the economic recovery, and unable to turn to the Chinese or Japanese to bail out the government,   the only course of action left will be for the Federal Reserve to "re-liquify" the market. That is, the Fed will simply 'print up' more money to use to buy the non-selling Treasury bills itself. And when this new money hits the marketplace, the amount of overall money in circulation will quickly increase.

The dictionary defines "inflation" as simply an increase in the money supply. When you increase the total amount of money -- but not correspondingly increase any more goods or services being produced -- the cost of everything you buy denominated in the unit of money (in this case, the dollar) will go up. It takes more of the pieces of paper called 'dollars' to buy the same goods and services.

Real wealth and hard-assets such as commodities (food, metals, gold) will go up in dollar terms. Other stronger currencies will go up too. Fixed-interest-rate loans (like 30-year fixed mortgages) will be a disaster for the lender and a magical liability for the borrower, who will be able to repay the loans years later in dollars that will be worth far less, if not worthless. Those lenders will be forced out of business by rising costs, reducing the supply of consumer and business credit even more.

This negative-reinforcing downward spiral, once started, cannot be easily stopped short of a massive depression. Interest rates could shoot up to 30-50% per year. In the worst-case scenario, hyperinflation, or monthly inflation above 50%, could occur. Such an event nearly always ends with a war or internal revolution.

The above scenario is what the strategic planners at the White House, the Treasury and the Federal Reserve desperately fear. And we are now likely on the knife edge, as Gerald Celente of Trends Research Institute has recently predicted.

I too, see this as an exceptional time. Fortunately, the White House is quite good at twisting both the arms of powerful people on Wall Street and Main Street. They've fired the Chairmen of General Motors and Chrysler and AIG. They've forced major solvent banks like Wells Fargo to take the so-called 'Tarp' bailout money even when they didn't need to and didn't want to. They've taken over 80% of all home mortgages with the nationalization of FreddyMac and FannieMae. And they've gotten gentle press treatment from those "main stream media" outlets (with the exception of CNBC's Rick Santelli).

I expect that the 3 New York-based bond rating agencies will go along with the US government and maintain the charade of its AAA rating for as long as possible, hoping that a miracle occurs and the fabled "green shoots" quickly grow into a sustained recovery, rather than a man-eating plant.

But I'm not optimistic, and I invite any reader to argue against my position. While I am hopeful in the future of humankind and the wonders that the free market and science can bring over the long term, in the short term I fear that the light I see at the end of this tunnel is, in fact, an oncoming train.

June 12, 2009

New 'Progressivism' is Statist Cancer Eating America's Soul

First nationalize the banks, next take over the industrial sector, and follow that with health care and energy...

Words matter. The way we describe ideas are more important still.

Take "Progressivism", for example. Progressivism is a form of "Corporatism". Some people call it "Statism". It is destroying our fundamental values of individual freedom and liberty. And like the family members who witness child abuse but deny it, we are still saying "it can't happen here". Psychiatrists are now warning about the similarities.

Progressives love tight top-down controls over all aspects of the society. There is government ownership, in conjunction with big-business - of the banking, insurance, financial, heavy-industry, and media sectors, but minus the heavy-handed suppression of popular dissent.

Progressivism was extremely popular with big-government proponents from both parties throughout the early 20th century. Many prominent Americans supported Progressivism after the Crash of '29 and throughout the Great Depression.

During the on-going financial crisis of the 20's and 30's, many people came to believe that the only way to recover from the collapse was to adopt massive doses of Keynesian economics and heavy-hand government control. It was a fool's errand.

Under President Franklin D. Roosevelt, Jr., the Congress became dominated by one party, the Supreme Court was notoriously stacked by the same party, and the president was re-elected for a total of 4 terms -- an event which had never before happened in the history of this country. The system of checks-and-balances had been suspended.

After FDR's death, the states enacted the XXII Amendment to the Constitution, prohibiting all future presidents from serving for more than two terms. On January 6, 2009, a bill was submitted in Congress to repeal the XXII Amendment. We may yet see a "President-for-life" if the new Progressives have their way.

Corporatism is a practice, "whereby a state, through the process of licensing and regulating officially-incorporated social, religious, economic, or popular organizations, effectively co-opts their leadership or circumscribes their ability to challenge state authority by establishing the state as the source of their legitimacy, as well as sometimes running them, either directly or indirectly through corporations."

Under Progressivism, which Teddy Roosevelt and Woodrow Wilson both praised, the duty of the government was to toss out the old dead Constitution from a previous era and introduce a new modern "living constitution", to re-mold America and reshape the morals and economy of the time.

Sound familiar?

In the dying days of the George W. Bush administration, Mr. Bush said, about our 230-year old capitalist country: "I've abandoned free-market principles to save the free market system". And so he had. He promptly bailed out the giant banks, insurance companies and car companies with initial down payments of taxpayer money. They were "too big to fail".

But common sense and Austrian economics say that this will ultimately fail. You must let the creative destruction of mismanaged and bloated companies by the market take place. Even if the cause of this crisis in the first place was decades-old government manipulation of the financial markets and union contract company regulation.

In the current administration, Progressivism has reached new heights. You can just hear 'ol Teddy Roosevelt (a Republican, by the way), saying "you get 'em!" "We need more government, bigger government, more control, less dissent, to fix our problems!"

And there always is a new problem to fix. It's even better if it's an emergency. Or as the White House's chief-enforcer and Chief-of-Staff Rahm Emanuel has said: "never let a serious crisis go to waste." Amen, brother. It's OK to pull out the stops in the housing crisis, the financial crisis, the unemployment crisis, and the auto manufacturing crisis.

Next will come the health care crisis, the energy crisis (good-bye 'big oil'), the media crisis (the government will issue 'licenses' to newspapers eligible for new bailout funds to prevent them from failing too. The fact that no one is reading what they're writing because it's more Progressive storytelling, makes it even more important to save their bacon).

Then, radio stations will be told to accept "local action committees", such as those formed by ACORN, to regulate the conservative talk radio commentators - off the air. Finally, the Internet will be licensed and controlled by the government. Filter technology such as that which American companies have installed in China will remove Inappropriate and dissenting views from reaching the Americans' eyeballs.

The "bi-partisan" bill which suppressed the first amendment rights of certain people to advertise their views just before an election was jointly written by Senators John McCain (R-AZ) and Russell Feingold (D-WI). It was duly upheld by the Supreme Court.

Wage controls, like those tried and failed by Richard Nixon, under the new "pay czar" will be expanded to apply to all people. Price controls on critical goods like milk and bread and gasoline will be expanded to all goods and services.

Look for more and more czars to run all aspects of your life.

The so-called "czars" are simply "Special Assistants to the President" - but they are not subject to advice and consent by the Senate and are arguably protected by "Executive Privilege" of the White House. Nice work if you can get it.

The net result of all this silliness, of course, is to distort the free marketplace to the extent that shortages will again appear everywhere, as they did at our service stations when Jimmy Carter issued his executive order to fix gas prices. And so will long lines to queue up for the pump - or the hospital.

Of course, those older people who are deemed to old to be "cured" will be denied life-saving procedures available to younger more desirable people such as kidney dialysis. This is not uncommon in other progressive socialist countries worldwide. After all, someone has to draw the line on these run-away costs. So, you can say goodbye to grandpa...

Meanwhile, the rest of the world will have likely advanced smartly ahead, not being cursed with this disease. China and India will continue to expand their GDP at furious rates, Russia will continue to sell ever more oil and natural gas to Western Europe - as it's principal supplier. And the world of "Chaostan" will continue to spin out crazies and fanatics who are against the free market values of toleration, individual liberty and respect for freedom that the United States was founded upon.

A free market must be just that. Free. Especially free of government control and manipulation. The government's job as an independent enforcer of the law is to do just that. It should not have a dog in that fight. When the government takes sides in the free market, it overwhelmingly sides with the producers against the consumers. Consumers crying out for government protection and revenge forget this fact.

Economics 101 teaches that each buyer and seller must be free of coercion when they trade in the marketplace. If they can't they're not free economically. And if you're not free economically, you can't be free politically. The market will just work - if it works at all.

But all of us will be poorer - both monetarily and spiritually. De Tocqueville warned us about how we could lose our "American Exceptionalism", as he called it in his book, Democracy in America. If you haven't flipped through it since high school, it's worth a re-read.

Bottom line. The U.S. is broke. We're paying our bills with IOU's. When that doesn't work, we just print up the money. In the meanwhile, every Progressive idea is being turned into law. More czars and bailouts -- and taxes -- are coming. You can count on a new hidden national sales tax of 15% or more to help "balance the budget". More regulations and controls mean less economic freedom.

It's all seems so obvious - unless you are a Progressive.

June 15, 2009

SECTION II
The American Economic System

JOIN, or DIE.

Some Useful Definitions

JOIN, or DIE.

Before one can jump into analyzing what's going on in the American economic system today, it's useful to synchronize our understandings of some basic concepts that most of us haven't thought about for a long time, if ever. We've had the marvelous luxury of not having to really worry about the economy and even the continuing existence of the United States itself, as we've come to know it.

But the time has now come to review and re-analyze our very core beliefs. What we know and what we believe will affect the future of America - and the entire world itself.

Modern "Progressivism", a form of liberal fascism with a "happy face" has been rapidly re-emerging in the 21st century United States. It is a cancer on the American soul which is systematically destroying the American Constitution and the economic system of the free-market and its entrepreneurial enterprise. What follows may become a history lesson in paradise lost.

Words matter.

To get a clear understanding of the meaning of our terminology, it is valuable to define some of the key terms that we are using. This way, we can proceed together, reading, as it were, from the same page.

The following definitions have been taken from the standard Webster's Dictionary (or Wikipedia when noted) with expanded commentary to clarify their usage.

NAKED:
Definition: Exposed, bare, unprotected

Synonyms: Open (undisguised, unadulterated, unadorned, stark, obvious, plain, simple)

MORALITY:
Definition: Concern with the distinction between good and evil or right and wrong; right or good conduct.

Synonyms: Ethics, Goodness (honesty, integrity, decency, virtue, godliness)

Commentary: . It is the internal mechanism which regulates our behavior towards others. "Absolute" or "Universal" morality is a fundamentally-held life position in which one's actions increase the happiness of anyone who lives by it, revolving around non-coercion toward others

ENTERPRENEUR:
Definition: A person who assumes the financial risk of the initiation, operation and management of a given business or undertaking.

Commentary: The way to become a successful entrepreneur is to serve others: "Find a Need and Fill it". In other words, give first and receive your reward later works in life as it does in love. The entrepreneur is a passionate and honest lover.

TORT: (from the Two Fundamental Laws)
Definition: Derived from the Latin word tortus which meant wrong. In French, "tort" means a wrong". Tort refers to that body of the law which will allow an injured person to obtain compensation from the person who caused the injury. Every person is expected to conduct themselves without injuring others. When they do so, either intentionally or by negligence, they can be required by a court to pay money to the injured party ("damages") so that, ultimately, they will suffer the pain cause by their action. Tort also serves as a deterrent by sending a message to the community as to what is unacceptable conduct.

CONTRACT: (from the Two Fundamental Laws)
Definition: An agreement entered into voluntarily between two or more persons.

A non-coercive agreement between two or more competent parties in which an offer is made and accepted, and each party benefits. The agreement can be formal, informal, written, oral or just plain understood. Some contracts are required to be in writing in order to be enforced. (2) An agreement between two or more parties which creates obligations to do or not do the specific things that are the subject of that agreement. Examples of a contract are a lease, a promissory note, or a rental agreement.

Commentary: For a contract to be legal, it must be agreed to without coercion being applied to either party. If a thief sticks a gun to your head and says "your money or your life", this is not a contract freely entered into by the hold-up victim.

CAPITALISM:
Definition: An economic system in which goods and services ("property") are produced, exchanged and owned by individuals with minimal governmental regulation.

Synonyms: Free Enterprise, Private Enterprise, Free Market, Entrepreneurship.

Both ethics (morality) and economics are intimately related. Both are concerned with human action: (1) personal conduct, and (2) personal decision, personal choice.

Capitalism may be subdivided into: (1) private property, (2) free markets, (3) competition, (4) division and combination of labor, and (5) social cooperation. They are mutually dependent. Private property means one's own personal property in consumption goods (such as a car, house, pair of shoes). It also means the private ownership of the "means of production".

Capitalism is unique in that it takes advantage of self-love and self-interest and harnesses them to production and exchange.

Or, as Adam Smith famously put it:

"The annual revenue of every society is always precisely equal to the exchangeable value of the whole annual produce of the industry, or rather is precisely the same thing with that exchangeable value. As every individual, therefore, endeavors as much as he can both to employ his capital in the support of domestic industry, and so to direct that industry that its produce may be of the greatest value; every individual necessarily labors to render the annual revenue of the society as great as he can. He generally, indeed, neither intends to promote the public interest, nor knows how much he is promoting it. By preferring the support of domestic to that of foreign industry, he intends only his own security; and by directing that industry in such a manner as its produce may be of the greatest value, he intends only his own gain, and he is in this, as in many other cases, led by an invisible hand to promote an end which was no part of his intention. Nor is it always the worse for the society that it was no part of it. By pursuing his own interest he frequently promotes that of the society more efficiently than when he really intends to promote it." (The Wealth of Nations, 1776).

In the Capitalist, or free-market system, the free individual is the centerpiece of society. Society forms voluntary groups to accomplish common goals for the specific interest of each member of the group. Coercion, either by armed thugs or the government is not allowed. A minimum government is established to accomplish only those things that it is recognized cannot be done by any voluntary group. These include national defense and, usually, the establishment of an independent court system operating under a tight "rule of law" to ensure that no one individual or group, including the government, can gain control of the free marketplace to the disadvantage of any other.

GOVERNMENT:
Definition: An organization of one or more people in control of the administrative apparatus of the STATE. The dominant decision-making and law-passing arm of the State.

Government is often confused with the State. They are not synonyms. A government can be fully voluntary in creation and operation. However, as most governments are usually in control of a "state" and exercise the powers of a state, they are often practically perceived as being interchangeable.

The STATE:

Definition: The State has been defined (by the renowned political economist Max Weber and later political philosophy) as the organization that holds a monopoly in the "legal" (legitimate) use of violence within its territory to enforce its laws over the people who live within its territory.

The State is the only collection of individuals which is not voluntary. It is, by definition, coercive. All other forms of human collective membership are voluntary. This includes churches, the workplace, sports & other clubs, schools (non-government), friendship societies and charities. Only through the ultimate barrel of a gun can the State enforce its laws on an individual.

Thus the State which intrudes the least on the personal liberties and individual freedoms of its citizens is the one which is the best: it is the one which does the least harm as it goes about its business of enforcing its laws.

The Just State is one which takes no side in a conflict between its citizens, administering its laws impartially and fairly. The unjust State is one in which everything has been criminalized, that is, every transgression of a law is a direct attack on the State itself and must be punished by imprisonment or death to the individual.

The State which has the most voluntary cooperation of its citizens is the one which is least feared. This State is usually constructed as a Democracy in which the individual citizens themselves have the ability through their collective vote to elect the members of the Government.

The bottom line: the smallest State does the least damage.

Winston Churchill observed: "It has been said that democracy is the worst form of government except all the others that have been tried."

TOTALITARIANISM:

Totalitarianism (or totalitarian rule) is a political system that, according to Wikipedia, "strives to regulate nearly every aspect of public and private life. Totalitarian regimes or movements maintain themselves in political power by means of an official all-embracing ideology and propaganda disseminated through the state-controlled mass media, a single party (usually) that controls the state, personality cults, control over the economy, regulation and restriction of free discussion and criticism, the use of mass surveillance", etc.

Benito Mussolini, the Italian dictator during WWII, popularized the concept of totalitarianism, and early 20th-century American Progressives like Presidents Woodrow Wilson and Franklin D. Roosevelt, Jr. were infatuated by it.

SOCIALISM:

Definition: A system of social organization by which the means of production and distribution ("property") are owned, managed, and controlled by the government, through the use of force.

Synonyms: Collectivism, Communism, Communalism, Marxism, Leninism, Maoism.

The French philosophers of the 18th Century - who were responsible for the revolt which launched the mass use of the Guillotine - launched an argument against private property using John Locke's theory of knowledge. (John Locke was the father of classical liberalism). They argued that everything that we are is simply a result of our experiences, not some fundamental set of universal truths. Thus, through new laws and state-run education human beings can be changed.

They theorized that property is the root of all evil, and therefore through its abolition people can be totally "socialized". People will then no longer desire to own anything, but will want to share everything. This became the basis of modern "socialism" as taught by Marx. For Marx, the definition of socialism or "communism" as he preferred to call it, was simply the abolition of all private property and its forced transfer to the State, a direct violation of both of the two fundamental Laws of Life.

"Force cannot change Right", Thomas Jefferson.

FASCISM:
"Fascism, is a radical and authoritarian nationalist political ideology and a Corporatist economic ideology" (Wikipedia definition).   While many people think of Fascism as a "right-wing" movement, it is, in fact a left-wing phenomena, a form of "Totalitarianism" akin to Socialism, or Marxism.

The full name of the German NAZI party was the: National Socialist German Workers Party". It was wildly admired by people on both sides of the Atlantic as a means of recovering from the "Great Depression", which began in 1929. Many prominent American figures were proponents of fascism being adopted in the United States, until just before the US was attacked by the Japanese at Pearl Harbor.

CORPORATISM:
Corporatism is defined by Wikipedia as: "a system of economic, political, and social organization where social groups or interest groups, such as business, ethnic, farmer, labor, military, or patronage groups, are joined together under a common governing jurisdiction to try to achieve societal harmony and promote coordinated development".

Corporatism is a practice, "whereby a state, through the process of licensing and regulating officially-incorporated social, religious, economic, or popular organizations, effectively co-opts their leadership or circumscribes their ability to challenge state authority by establishing the state as the source of their legitimacy, as well as sometimes running them, either directly or indirectly through corporations."

"Liberal Fascism" is often thought of as a form of friendly Corporatism. That is, it is "fascism light" with tight top-down control over all aspects of the society, government ownership, in conjunction with big-business of the banking, insurance, financial, heavy-industry, and media sectors, without the "boot jack" suppression of the popular descent that the NAZI form of Fascism was famous for.

The Two Fundamental Laws of Life

A "Model" is the way we construct our internal understanding of how the world works. It is our belief system which grounds our spiritual center. It provides people with a sort of "Universal Truth" that we live by, and expect others to live by as well.

Our American Model of Universal Truth, is enshrined in the Declaration of Independence, which states in its second paragraph that: "We hold these Truths to be self-evident, that all Men are created equal, that they are endowed by their Creator with certain unalienable Rights, that among these are Life, Liberty, and the Pursuit of Happiness".

Our Founding Fathers believed that one's Happiness was the highest Right that we could aspire to obtain.

Over the centuries there have been many models which various philosophers have proposed to explain how "the world works".

Most models are proven false for several reasons:

1) they violate the underlying "laws of nature", that is they are contrary to how things actually work or are physically programmed to work, either by the laws of physics or our DNA coding, and

2) they have been shown to fail when put into "real world" practice and tested.

A few have survived because of their universal truth.

The United States uses the two fundamental principles of the old British common law as the legal model for our Constitution.

These are:

(1) Do all you have agreed to do.
This is the basis of contract law.

(2) Do not encroach on other persons or their property.

This is the basis of tort law and some criminal law.

These are the two laws taught by all religions, which is why they were the basis of common law--the law common to all. They form the basis for a "Universal Truth".

When the two fundamental laws are not widely obeyed, the only options are tyranny or chaos.

Travel around the world. You will find that countries in which these laws are most closely obeyed by the people and the governments are the ones with the most liberty, prosperity and peace.

The American legal model attempts to encapsulate and codify these universal truths. However, since power always corrupts, the Founding Fathers designed the United States Constitution to do three further things:

1) cripple the power of the State by keeping it small and starving it of money (e.g. direct income tax was unconstitutional for the first 140 years),

2) prevent any one person or group seizing control of the State by installing a set of checks and balances, and

3) define and codify a Bill of Rights to protect its citizens from the power of the   State to be used against them and to limit the State's powers to only those described within the four corners of the written Constitution document.

In doing so, they intentionally created a Republic, not a Democracy, recognizing as historian Alexander Fraser Tyler observed, "A democracy . . . can only exist until a majority of voters discover that they can vote themselves largesse from the public treasury."

Alexander Hamilton wrote, "We are now forming a republican form of government. Real liberty is not found in the extremes of democracy . . . . If we incline too much to democracy, we shall soon shoot into a monarchy, or some other form of dictatorship."

The Constitution therefore states, "The United States shall guarantee to every State in this Union a Republican Form of Government . . . ."

This provided the foundation for a government of limited power whose principal obligation is to protect the rights and liberties of the people.

This charter of power from the people was not intended to be changed easily or to be a "living document," subject to the whim of the moment. After the Constitutional Convention of 1787, Benjamin Franklin, when asked what had been wrought, responded, "A republic, sir, if you can keep it."

Richard Maybury is the Publisher of the Early Warning Report, which tracks the battle between the free world and "Chaostan" as he calls it. (see: www:chaostan.com). He refers to the two fundamental laws as the basis of his entire understanding of 5000 years of world history. He has been studying the application and effect of the two fundamental laws his entire life.

It's worth quoting him and giving him credit here for his clear understanding.

As Mr. Maybury sees it: "these laws are essential for an advanced society. The first gives rise to trade and specialization of labor. The second creates peace, security and goodwill.

Many animals are social. Wolves, ants, chimpanzees and whales come to mind. Each social species has laws for social conduct coded into their DNA. These laws exist to promote the well-being of the species.

When a member of a wolf pack violates a law he is punished by other members of the pack. If violation of the rules is widespread, the whole pack is punished by nature. The pack ceases to operate harmoniously, food becomes difficult to acquire and members die. Humans have more free will than other species and therefore more ability for individuals to violate laws, but the laws are there, in our DNA. These laws are higher than any human law, and human law cannot repeal them.

When these laws are violated, the result is some kind of damage to someone. Good intentions do not prevent this damage, nor do euphemisms. When stealing is called a tax, it remains stealing and it is every bit as damaging. Widespread violation of the laws by anyone, including a government, causes damage until the civilization collapses and the survivors, if any, must start over, as in Europe's Dark Ages. "

His excellent monthly newsletter is required reading for everyone concerned with the American trends of the next 20 years - as a result of following or ignoring the two fundamental laws. Quoting Richard Maybury once again, "Liberty is the source of prosperity".

A Moral Economic System:
Austrian Economics

JOIN, or DIE.

An economic system is the result of its legal system.

Economic systems vary between those in which the individual is king to those in which the state is king. In other words, they can be constructed as systems in which economic power comes from the grass roots up or from the top controller down.

The best economic model is "Austrian Economics", which represents the most free market economic understanding of human interaction. It also appears to be most in tune with the understandings of the Declaration of Independence and our constitutional structure of "checks and balances". It is a model which encourages competition and discourages corruption.

Its founders were from Austria, including Ludwig Von Mises and F.A. Hayek, who received the Nobel Prize in 1974. The "Chicago School" of Economics as represented by Milton Friedman (1976 Nobel Prize in Economics) and numerous Austrian School "think tanks" such as the Heritage Foundation (www.heritage.org), the CATO Institute (www.cato.org) and the Hoover Institution (www.hoover.stanford.edu) continue on this tradition.

Every year the Heritage Foundation, in conjunction with the Wall Street Journal, publishes its Index of Economic Freedom based primarily on the application of this universal truth country-to-country.

An excellent Austrian School source for further information is The Foundation for Economic Education (www.fee.org).

FEE maintains an extensive web site and publishes books and articles both on-line and in printed form. Frederic Bastiat's short book, The Law, is a must-read for those who want to understand clearly what makes the Law just and a society, in turn, moral. Leonard Read's I, Pencil, is a short essay on how the lowly pencil comes into existence because of the coordinated entrepreneurial efforts of thousands of people in dozens of industries throughout the world.

The Basis of Property: Its Hierarchy & Rights

All living creatures are extremely acquisitive and territorial. Deer fight battles for territory; a female won't mate with a male who has no territory. The male must be "rich" in territory or she can't raise her family.

Human beings share this same hard-coded DNA to own "property" (territory). Even among children raised in the experimental youth camps of the USSR or the Israeli socialist Kibbutz, one of the first words that children learn is "mine".

Acknowledging this innate natural law of property, Laws are established by the civil government to recognize the existence of property and to establish a set of just rules to recognize the ownership of property. This includes its creation, transfer, use & destruction, and the contractual relationship between different parties to the same property (such as a renter and a landlord, or an automobile manufacturer and its driver-owner, or a software programmer and its licensee-user).

Property "rights" flow from the individual's ownership, top-down, of the 3 kinds of property that exist for human beings. They are:

1) First Cause or "Primordial" Property: (the highest property right)

Your own life – and its physical possession (by you)

A Just (or Moral) Society bans: a) slavery, b) the draft

2) Primary Property:

Your ideas – the fruit of your own mental thoughts

A Just Society recognizes intellectual property rights such as: a) copyright, b) patent, c) trademark, d) trade secrets & processes

3) Secondary Property:

Your "value added" work – the fruit of your own actions

A Just Society recognizes ownership of things: a) real property (land & buildings), b) machinery and human artifacts, c) abstract creations (stocks & bonds), d) other inventions of the human mind

Over the past ten thousand years of human existence, both philosophers and ordinary folk have recognized the natural order of property and its rights. The old Mesopotamia tablets dug up at the gates of Babylon show property contracts between buyers and sellers. These predate the Hebrews and their Bible by thousands of years.

Government Ownership of the "Means of Production" in the USA Today: a "Mixed Bag"

JOIN, or DIE.

Forms of government range from totally individual-oriented free-market (capitalist) to totally government-oriented totalitarian (communist, socialist or fascist). The libertarian test for freedom is simply: is the government part of the problem or part of the solution? Does its existence increase my personal liberty and freedoms or decrease them?

Using this criteria, the United States today is a mixed-economy. It is part free-market (capitalist) and part socialist (communist). It is easy to demonstrate this.

Simply consider what the "government" owns today:

Post Office (25% of all civilian federal workers). Alternatives: FedEx, UPS, DHL, others

...and at the Federal, State & Local levels:

Electric Companies & Nuclear Power Generating Plants (e.g. TVA)
Water Companies (e.g. San Francisco's Hetch Hetchy System)
Sewage Systems
Waste Removal
Fire Companies
Police Departments
Gas Companies
Ports & Airports
Air Traffic Control Centers
Train Companies

Telephone Companies
Cable TV Companies
Bus Lines
Boats & Ferry Lines
Bridges, Tunnels & Roads (both free and toll)
Space Vehicle Launching Systems & satellites
Armament Manufacturers (e.g. armories)
Nuclear Fuel Manufacturing Plants
Hospitals (e.g. Veterans Administration) & Research abs
Office Buildings & Apartments (General Services Administration GSA)
Museums, Parks, Zoos, Libraries, Ball Parks, Exhibition & Performance Halls
Forests & Logging Operations
Schools: primary, secondary, high school, college & university
Radio & TV Stations (e.g. Voice of America)
Printing & Publishing (e.g. General Printing Office GPO)
Enforcement Officers (Armed), including: Army, Air Force, Navy, Marines, TSA, etc.
Land (70% of all land west of the Rocky Mountains)

Recently, the United States has moved further toward the process of extending government control either indirectly or directly over a far greater segment of the private sector. Nationalization, either through controlling loans or stock ownership (preferred or common shares) has enabled the federal government to own or partially own:

Major federally-chartered banks like CitiBank
Major insurance companies like AIG
General Motors and other automobile-industry companies.

Proposed government nationalization of other sectors include the health care industry and the energy industry, as well as federal government expansion of national control over the independent states through the use of loan guarantees (California) and other "guarantees" of debt, using the ability of the US Treasury to issue more Treasury Bills (IOU's) which the Federal Reserve then buys up with printing-press fiat money.

By using the power of government domain coupled with the power of sovereign (monopoly) issued money, the process of moving from a freer independent economy to more controlled "corporatist" economy can be accelerated. This strategy was proposed at the turn of the 20th century by Presidents Teddy Roosevelt and Woodrow Wilson, a Republican and Democrat, respectively.

Both were Progressives, a political movement which espoused powerful central government and central control and/or ownership of the means of production in conjunction with large corporations. Modern "progressives" support a form of "liberal fascism", or fascism with a happy face, as described by Jonah Goldberg in his best-selling book, Liberal Fascism. Perhaps this brand of friendly politically-correct fascism is most like Peronism, formulated by the Argentina President Juan Peron as a populist movement.

The systematic reduction of the free market economy and the increase of state-owned businesses results, of course, in a collapse of GDP, decrease in individual liberties - especially among those minority populations opposed to the government's controls and policies, and civil strife ending in military dictatorship. This is one of the universally consistent outcomes of ultimate conversion of a mixed-economy to a state-dominated or controlled economy.

The Naked Moral Entrepreneur

JOIN, or DIE.

Introduction

The Naked Moral Entrepreneur.

Is there such a beast? How do we know one when we see one? Are they gradually becoming extinct or they now breeding like rabbits?

What makes up a "Naked Moral Entrepreneur"? Why is he important?

What is an Entrepreneur? And what is his moral code of ethics?

Many people believe that for a society to be successful, there has to be a strong free market system operating in a strong moral culture. I believe that this is a necessary but not sufficient condition.

The second condition is the creation of a culture of entrepreneurship. This is a willingness to take risks to find and create a product or service that the marketplace wants to buy. In other words, to make the better mousetrap. First, the entrepreneur contributes to society with a new invention, process, perhaps a new life-saving drug or process. Then, if he is very lucky, the entrepreneur is rewarded by the marketplace's only reward mechanism, the payment of money (hopefully lots) from happy, satisfied and grateful consumers.

But before the first mark 1.0 mousetrap appears in the marketplace, the entrepreneur must have the vision to see that such a need exists - before the consumer (and especially before possible competitors) recognizes he wants one. This foresight is the magic which separates the true entrepreneur from the me-too follower.

Being an entrepreneur is a risky business. Most people given the choice between freedom and safety elect to go for safety. This is why most people work for another person for their living. Being an entrepreneur is scary stuff - and the driving force of the entrepreneur is mostly found in the small mom-and-pop or start-up business.

It is the magic which can only function in a free market economy.

To be the inventor of the iPod or the iPhone means that the product must be invented and manufactured before it can be sold. Thus, in a modern economy, economists point out that it is, in fact, the producer who drives the market, not the consumer. It is the producer who creates the wealth - which often emerges as an idea from the mind of the entrepreneur. The statement often quoted in the popular media, that the US consumer accounts for 70% of the GDP is, in fact, false.

Statement: It is the role of the Entrepreneur to maximize Happiness.

It is the role of the Entrepreneur to "find a need and fill it", that is, to find out what people (the marketplace) want and then to provide them with the solution (the good or service). In other words, to find out what will make them "happy". This is the ultimate Entrepreneur's joy.

The old Soviet joke: "They pretend to pay us and we pretend to work" is doubly funny. First, because of its obvious joke that no one works, and second because of the much more subtle observation that the hierarchy of a government-owned communist system is "bass-ackwards": namely that in the real world, first you must give something to society (your work effort) and only then do you get rewarded for it (you get paid).

The Entrepreneur is the Everyman or Everywoman. He is an expert at all things. He must be familiar with sales & marketing, financing & accounting, manufacturing & production, research, personal, and the law. He must be a dreamer, a person driven to excellence, a risk taker.

The Entrepreneur is passionate. He has a passion for his idea, his creation, his invention, his dream, his vision. He lives for a cause. He is driven. He often works 80 hours a week or more. To him, however, he is having the most fun of his life. He is playing. He is creating. He is happy.

If the Entrepreneur builds that "better mousetrap" that everyone wants to have, then he will be rewarded for his passion by that fundamental means by which other people can show their appreciation: they will give him money for it.

The Entrepreneur has long been recognized as being a "breed apart". Successful entrepreneurs have a high propensity to make decisions on their own, to be action-oriented, to assume risk, and to persevere in the face of uncertainty and adversity. In other words, the Entrepreneur exhibits a high degree of individualism.

Thus it becomes obvious that the Entrepreneur can only exist freely in a free market or Capitalist society. (Entrepreneurs are usually deemed to be enemies of the people in Communist or Marxist societies. The most talented flee or are shot or become black-market traders).

In a Baylor University study, researchers Justin Longenecker, Joseph McKinney and Carlos Moore found that Entrepreneurs exhibit a more stringent standard of ethics, particularly when the decisions involve individual courage. Their study further found that Entrepreneurs as a class were more able to perceive moderate or extreme pressure to engage in unethical behavior then the average person.   Finally, they discovered in a later study of ten thousand individuals that Entrepreneurs that have strong religious faith have higher ethical standards that the class of Entrepreneurs in general. These results are not surprising.

Some observers have defined two fundamental "archetypes" that people self-select:

Type I people are those who first minimize their risks and then maximize their rewards. These people usually opt for safety and security instead of freedom. They usually work for other people. In the extreme they are renters; they rarely own their own houses. They look to their parents and then later to the government to coddle and protect them. They are often afraid and fearful of external events outside their control.

Recent polls taken in Russia indicate that well over 80% of the population considers itself in this first camp. They have indicated that they are want to have more security at the cost of giving up their personal freedoms - even if this includes the right to vote for their government leaders.

Type II people are those who first maximize their potential profits (or rewards) and then strive to minimize their risks. They usually opt for liberty and freedom instead of safety and security. "Damn the torpedoes – full steam ahead!" (Admiral David Farragut, Civil War). "Give Me Liberty or Give Me Death" (Patrick Henry).

They become the great artists like the Impressionists who were outcasts in their early days. Or independent film makers like George Lucas who created Star Wars because the big-business bureaucrats could not accept his vision.

Or they became inventors like Alexander Graham Bell who - when he presented his new-fangled telephone to Western Union's president, William Orton - was summarily rejected that the world's largest and most powerful corporation wasn't interested in "a toy!".

American has been and continues to be the world's breeding ground for Type II people.

The Entrepreneur represents the extreme risk-taking personality. The lawyer represents the most risk-adverse personality. The good entrepreneur surrounds himself with the best attorneys...

There are more people who want to be Entrepreneurs in America today then there have ever been in the history of the country. And the irony is that most people who "become their own bosses" ultimately succeed in both being freer (and happier) and more secure (and richer) then their Type I neighbors.

Entrepreneurs and innovators thrive in a contractual society, that is a society governed by the rule of law and which has strong property rights. They feel ill at ease if decisions about their life and their work are made by a dictator or government bureaucrat.

The Entrepreneur is the catalyst between labor and capital. The Capitalist or Free-Market system recognizes the value of the Entrepreneur in making the necessary innovations that move the society ahead.

In Marxist theory such a role is non-existent. To adopt the socialist "solution" to a society, that is, to make "labor" (as represented by the government commissar) as the owner of the capital destroys the Entrepreneur in the equation. For labor in the role of wage-earner (and risk-avoider) always gets the upper hand over labor in the role of guardian of capital and entrepreneurial risk-taker.

In these systems, the fundamental laws of both economics and morality are violated:

1) there is no relationship between what something costs and what it sells for,

2) there is no relationship between supply and demand,

3) there is no relationship between time and money, and

4) paper to the bureaucrat is more important that the individual person ("let me   see your papers, please!).

The Systems Model of Life

In the Systems Model of an organism (or a machine or a human-created organization), there is an Input, An Output, a System (the box which processes the input and puts out the output), and a Feedback loop. The entire organism exists within an external Environment, the "soup" which supports its life.

The personal computer can be thought of as a System.

It has Inputs (from the Mouse, Keyboard, Camera, Scanner, other sensors), Outputs (the display, printer, voice response, other devices), a System (the computer processor), a Feedback Loop (if it doesn't do what we tell it to do we kick it or reprogram it) and an external Environment (which may be a room where lots of other similar Systems are at work, perhaps doing overlapping or even competitive work).

The modern entrepreneurial business can also be thought of as a System.

It has Inputs in the form of people (labor), money (capital), commodities, ideas (intellectual property including the design of the business itself), and buyers. It has Outputs in the form of goods or services, money, ideas, etc. The System takes the Inputs and transforms them through its value-adding processes to create Outputs. A Feedback Loop continuously works to provide the system with some balance. Via the Feedback Loop the System can understand what effects its Outputs have on its Inputs and its Environment. Via the Feedback Loop, too, the Environment can provide further input to the System.

When an organism becomes so big that it becomes a significant percentage of and ultimately takes over its environment, squeezing all other organisms out, the organism is said to be a "cancer". The ultimate solution for such a dysfunctional organism is its death.

When a man-made system such as a company grows so big that it becomes a significant percentage of its environment, it ultimately begins to confuse its environment with itself. Thus you have absurd statements, such as the one made in Senate hearings in 1955 by Charlie Wilson, then chairman of General Motors, "What's good for General Motors is good for the rest of America".

Clearly GM had gotten confused. Because it confused itself with its environment and its customers, it was unprepared to deal with the influx of Japanese and European automobile manufacturers like Toyota and Volkswagen which destroyed its market share – and almost the company itself – within a matter of decades.

The lesson for the Entrepreneur? He is part of an organic whole. The Entrepreneur exists in a marketplace environment with feedback ever present. The successful entrepreneur must always be true to his own moral code of ethics while always listening to his customers' feedback.

The Organization as Entrepreneur

Entrepreneurship is easy to recognize when we see it, but it is difficult to define formally. We might see it as a dynamic integration of four elements:

(1) the development of marketable innovations,

(2) the charisma to attract capital for their exploration,

(3) the leadership to organize labor and technology for their production, and

(4) the marketing skills to distribute and sell them.

Each element may be well known by itself, but their integration is a harder to achieve.

As Swedish Sociologist Hans L. Zetterberg points out:

"Organizational entrepreneurship on a large scale is a characteristic of today's post-industrial societies. Such entrepreneurship has many advantages over the personal variety that has dominated in the past and still is growing in many less developed countries. Organizational entrepreneurship can span generations without the threats to continuity posed by the whims of inheritance in selecting successors. It can handle a larger number of marketable innovations at the same time, making sure that new ones enter the market as old ones become obsolete. It is not barred from production requiring high initial investments. It can handle long and complex productions and is not overly dependent on quick sales. It can afford and encourage the training and specialization of its employees."

The appearance of marketable innovations within the large

business establishments in an affluent society is not a matter of chance, nor is it dependent on a flash of genius. It is the result of a much more orderly, more pedestrian process. A most remarkable achievement of the modern entrepreneur is the creation of organizations in which the development of innovations is routine.

Dr. Zetterberg observes:

"The main bench marks in the process of developing marketable innovations are well known:

(1) Long-range planning enables a corporation to gauge the need for new products   and markets and spreads an awareness of this through the ranks of the corporation.

(2) There is a separate budgeting of time, money, and man-hours for innovations inside the firm and for the procurement of marketable ideas from outside.

(3) An established routine provides for impartial evaluation of innovative   concepts and for the setting of priorities among them according to how well they   suit the firm's marketing and level of technology as well as their estimated impact on the market.

(4) Test production and trial marketing are managed by a special organizational unit.

Corporations adopting these procedures retain their old concern for volume and quality of production while adding a new concern for novelty and change.

Experience shows that these two fields of endeavor need to be demarcated. The research and development budget must be separate from the production budget. The developers should not be personnel borrowed from production and liable to be recalled to their old jobs to handle crises there. Management of production should be separate from management of research and development, for no day-to-day production manager can be expected to have the time or motivation to develop innovations that would render obsolete the very process he is managing.

Du Pont's development of Nylon, Bell Telephone's development of the transistor, the bubble memory, and the laser, Battelle's development of the xerographic process were all done in separate laboratories; in the case of xerography Battelle in fact was an outside laboratory commissioned to do the work. Xerox was the result.

Management backed these inventions not because they were technological miracles - the world is full of technological miracles - but because management believed that these inventions would have a tremendous impact on the market.

In innovation-prone corporations top management should ideally act like the controller in an airport tower and usher in one innovation after another in an orderly fashion. This is the ideal."

One of the best examples of such an innovation-driven entrepreneurial company is Minnesota Mining and Manufacturing, known worldwide simply as 3M, the inventor of Scotch tape and Post-It Notes and thousands of other well known and not so well known products and processes. 3M is the literal entrepreneurial invention factory gone wild.

Entrepreneurial organizations do not flourish well under a heavy-handed government. The process of free-thinking, innovating for what the consumer wants to buy in the marketplace, is replaced by politically-mandated commands as to what the politician thinks is "good" for the society. Usually, this means pandering to the special interest lobby groups which support the politician in his or her next election campaign.

The classic free-market idea to "build a better mousetrap and the world will beat a path to your door" becomes trumped by the organization's raw survival needs. Build what the government dictates - or suffer the consequences.

Of course, such a society rapidly deteriorates into a type of government-controlled corporatism. In this system, bigger is better. And controlled or outright owned by the government is better still. Eventually, the system becomes totally corrupted and degenerates into a form of state-run totalitarianism popularly known as fascism.

Smaller organizations, if allowed to survive, are tightly regulated and taxed. Innovation is crushed under the boot of state control and political expediency, often masquerading as "political correctness".

Ultimately, systems theory points out that once the bloated government becomes an overwhelming percentage of the overall society, the living organism becomes corrupted with a toxic cancer and ultimately dies, as the entrepreneurial DNA of a free-market is damaged beyond repair. The end-game of such a system usually degenerates into a war.

Either an external war is conjured into existence, designed to enable the current politicians to stay in power under the rubric "your country right or wrong", because one can't possibly "throw the rascals out" in a time of national emergency.

Or, a full-blown civil war erupts between the political and social elites and the people. This can take the form of a peaceful Gandhi-like revolution, where political cartoons showing the naked emperor spring up and the people begin to laugh at the ruling class, or it can become violent.

Fundamental work on the dynamics of the entrepreneurial organization has been done to analyze the phenomena of the successful entrepreneurial company. A leaders in this field is Swedish Sociologist Hans L. Zetterberg (www.Zetterberg.org), for which credit of much of the above is due.

So, organizations, like people, can maintain entrepreneurial spirit, but only if centered in a firm free-market system which follows the two fundamental laws.

The Two Types of
Big Organizational Structures

JOIN, or DIE.

There are two types of big organizational structures on earth today:

1) those that get their resources (wealth) from taxation,

and,

2) those that get their resources (wealth) from profits.

Both can be entrepreneurial. Both can be important, even vital to a society. The maintenance of a national army and justice system provide for the security of the overall free-market society.

However, the first organization operates as a drain on the productive wealth of the society as the application of taxation removes money from the pockets of the people or the producers which could otherwise be spent on other more productive areas.

Taxation acts as a kind of brake on the productive output of society and causes mal-direction of investment from the free-market choice to the politically-made choice. It encourages "gaming" the system by special-interest groups which buy the votes of the politicians through lobbying efforts for the special-interest goals.

The quid-pro-quo, of course, is the guarantee by the special interest lobbyists to fund the re-election campaigns of the politicians in return for the special interest legislation which benefit them and suppresses their competition.

The second enterprise, the private-sector organization, creates the real wealth in an economy which is an expanding pie. In a free market system, both the buyer and seller benefit and both are richer for the trade which takes place. It is only in a government-controlled socialist or Marxist system that the pie is seen as fixed, and must be "fairly" shared by everyone. The fallacy of this argument is shown in every Econ 101 Macroeconomics class taught today.

So can governments be entrepreneurial in spirit?

Not usually. But if they rigidly adhere to the two fundamental principles and the understanding of the Bill of Rights (designed to protect the people from an out-of-control government), it may be possible. The gating principle is the supremacy of the individual, not the state. Sadly, most politicians readily succumb to the siren song of the government power trap, which they can easily fall into. Using the populist "progressive" slogan: "I'm from the government and I'm here to help you" can easily sway the unthinking individual who forgets the adage that "there's no such thing as a free lunch" and ignores the ultimate price of loss of personal freedom as restrictions, controls, norms and beliefs are then mandated from the top down.

The Entrepreneur in Action

JOIN, or DIE.

- In Human Action, Ludwig von Mises wrote:

"The direction of all economic affairs is, in the market society, a task of the entrepreneurs. Theirs is the control of production. They are at the helm and steer the ship. A superficial observer would believe that they are supreme. But they are not. They are bound to obey unconditionally the captain's orders. The captain is the consumer. Neither the entrepreneurs nor the farmers nor the capitalists determine what has to be produced. The consumers do that. If a businessman does not strictly obey the orders to the public as they are conveyed to him by the structure of market prices, he suffers losses, he goes bankrupt, and is thus removed from his eminent position at the helm."

- George Reisman has argued that racial segregation would rapidly disappear under a truly free market run by the Entrepreneur-businessman:

"The businessman seeking profit is vitally dependent on the patronage of customers. This dependency is expressed in such popular sayings as "the customer is king" and "the customer is always right." Blacks are customers, and, as they rose economically, would be more and more important customers. It is absurd to believe that businessmen would want to turn customers away by denying them access to their premises or humiliating them with such requirements as separate drinking fountains."

However the above belief in the Entrepreneur's ultimate respect for his customer is challenged by some.

The Objectivist Center (www.objectivistcenter.org), the organization dedicated to continuing the ideas of Ayn Rand (see also the Ayn Rand Institute at www.aynrand.org), poses the following questions:

"But evil men can be as true to their values as good men are to theirs. And if any two sayings do not characterize Howard Roark (the hero of Atlas Shrugged) , they are "the customer is king" and "the customer is always right.""

"So which virtue shall we claim for capitalism? That its producers are free to stick by their values, despite the demands of consumers? Or that producers will overlook all rational and irrational distinctions among people and products in pursuit of money? And if we claim the former, but not the latter, what becomes of our claim that capitalism provides the market with ever-shifting, and always efficient flows of production and capital.

• The economist Israel Kirzner wrote about "Entrepreneurial Discovery and the Law of Supply and Demand." in Freeman: Ideas on Liberty, the journal of the Foundation for Economic Education.

There, he laid out a picture of the Entrepreneur in the free market that emphasized how the Entrepreneur thinks:

"The successful businessman-entrepreneur 'sees' what other market participants have not yet seen; the entrepreneur sees opportunities to buy at one price and to sell at a higher price. To see such opportunities will typically call for (a) superior imagination and vision (since the perceived opportunity to sell at the higher price is likely to exist only in the future) and (b) creativity (since such a profit opportunity is likely to take the form of selling what one buys in innovatively different form, and/or different place, than was relevant at the time of purchase"

"Entrepreneurs act imaginatively and creatively, seeking to identify and to grasp market profit opportunities (generated by earlier entrepreneurial limitations of vision). As a result of the interplay of such entrepreneurial acts of vision, product prices and quantities of product offered for sale tend to be nudged systematically in the direction of the market-clearing price/quantity configuration."

"The American Creed"

Many decades ago, the American Creed was written by Dean Alfange, an American statesman born December 2, 1899, in Constantinople (now Istanbul). He was raised in upstate New York and went on to obtain his degree in law from Columbia University, and later taught at the University of Massachusetts.

In 1942, he was the labor party candidate for Governor or New York.

"I do not choose to be a common man. It is my right to be uncommon--if I can.

I seek opportunity--not security. I do not wish to be a kept citizen, humbled and dulled by having the state look after me.

I want to take the calculated risk, to dream and to build, to fail and to succeed.

I refuse to barter incentive for a dole.

I prefer the challenges of life to the guaranteed existence, the thrill of fulfillment to the stale calm of utopia.

I will not trade freedom for beneficence or my dignity for a handout.

I will never cower before any master nor bend to any threat.

It is my heritage to stand erect, proud, and unafraid, to think and act for myself, enjoy the benefits of my creations and to face the world boldly and say, this I have done.

All this is what it means to be an American."

The American Creed is, in fact, the creed of the American Entrepreneur. Perhaps the culture of America gives birth to the Entrepreneur. Certainly it can be argued that the greatest collection of Entrepreneurs that the world has seen have come from the United States.

Dr. Douglas B. Rasmussen, Professor of Philosophy, St. John's University, New York, has described the American Creed and the underlying foundation of the free individual:

"Here are some of the basic truths that seem to be expressed in, implied, or at least suggested by this poem which was widely taught in the 1950's.

1. The ultimate source of wealth—both economically and morally—is found in the human intellect. Neither the economic capital for material prosperity nor the moral capital for human flourishing can exist without the human mind discovering and making actual the potentialities that nature in general and human nature in particular provide. Without the exercise of the human intellect, no wealth of any form can actually exist.

2. The intellectual insight that is necessary for an entrepreneur to see an opportunity for profit and create wealth is the same insight that is needed for an individual to put together a life in which final goods and virtues are discovered, achieved, maintained, and appropriately enjoyed.

3. This intellectual insight is an exercise of practical reason, which does not occur automatically or without effort. It is something that only the individual human being can initiate and maintain. It cannot be provided by others. It is a self-directed act.

4. When this intellectual insight is appropriately exercised, it is an exercise of the intellectual virtue of practical wisdom, and it involves such moral virtues as temperance, integrity, and honesty. It calls forth the ideal of human excellence, of human flourishing, of self-perfection.

5. The creation of material wealth is one of the necessary final goods of human perfection or flourishing. So, not only is it not wrong to create wealth or profit, it is in fact something that any and every human being needs to pursue. It is something that is good for human beings and ought to be done.

6. The creation of wealth, just like any of other basic goods that constitute human flourishing, must be achieved in an appropriate manner. Here is the wisdom of Aristotle's "doctrine of the mean."

7. Yet, what is often forgot when it comes to the doctrine of the mean is Aristotle's words, "the mean relative to us." Thus, finding what is appropriate amounts to finding what the appropriate balance or weighting of basic goods is for one as an individual human being. Each of us has our own unique potentialities that need to be made actual. There is no abstract rationalistic recipe or standard or plan here. (Such rationalistic procedures work, by the way, for neither persons nor economies.) So, we truly need to fashion our own unique forms of flourishing, and this comes with respect to how to balance and integrate all the goods and virtues of human life, including wealth. Each of us needs to, in the words of the poem: be uncommon, if we can.

8. None of these activities are done in isolation but always with and among others. We are social animals from the very beginning to the very end; and since we are not limited to any one form of social life, our sociality is ultimately cosmopolitan in nature. We are open to relationships with all of human-kind. We are part of what Hayek called, "the Great Society."

9. For each of us to pursue our own form of flourishing in the great society, we need to create a social and political context whose basic structural principles do not, as a matter or principle, prejudice that context more toward one form of flourishing over any other. We need a context that respects our potential for individuality and our uncommon forms of excellence.

10. As a result, we need a political/legal order whose struc-

tural principles protect that which is both common and peculiar to every person's form of human flourishing—that is, self-direction.

11. Each of us and every one of us needs to have the possibility of self-direction protected, and the protection of this possibility allows for a political/legal order that is not structurally prejudiced

12. Such a political/order is one whose foundational principles are the basic negative rights to life, liberty, and property.

13. Such a political/legal order does not make virtue or human flourishing its aim. It aspires only to protect liberty and thereby the condition by which it is possible for human beings to be moral agents—namely, self-direction.

14. Given that human flourishing is unique, social, and self-directed, protecting liberty is all to which the political/legal order either ought or can aspire. To aspire for more is both moral folly and rationalistic hubris.

15. Yet, reality is knowable, and though it does not guarantee success in life, it allows, for the most part, ample opportunity for people to find fulfillment, if they will but exercise the effort to use their minds and develop the appropriate virtues, and if we make sure not to create a political/legal order whose structural conditions fail to protect liberty. We need to protect the possibility of self-direction; for that is necessary for the economic and moral entrepreneurship required for material prosperity, human flourishing, and civil society.

Overall, a world in which entrepreneurs are praised for their virtues and creativity is a world of greater material and moral prosperity. It is a world in which moral virtues are present, but it is also a world that requires that liberty be seen as the paramount value of the political/legal order. Yet, the basis for this is a certain moral and cultural climate—namely, one that recognizes the moral imperative of each of us discovering and achieving our own unique form of human excellence or flourishing."

References & Resources

JOIN, or DIE.

For the interested reader, a rich collection of resources are available to inspire, teach, caution and explore the entrepreneur, natural law, the free enterprise system, and the American governmental design.

For a running commentary of the economic world we now live in, the good the bad and the ugly, see in particular my on-going columns in HumanEvents.org.

A. Recommended Web Sites:

www.Heritage.org
The Heritage Foundation. (also www.TownHall.com)

www.CATO.org
The CATO Foundation

www.FEE.org
The Foundation for Economic Education

www.Mises.org
The Ludwig Von Mises Institute

www.LibertyHaven.org
No longer active. But you can, in particular, see their primer on Austrian Economics at http://web.archive.org/web/20061205223721/www.libertyhaven.com/theoreticalorphilosophicalissues/austrianeconomics/index.html

B. Books & Papers:

The Law, Frederic Bastiat, FEE Books, with expanded commentary (books@fee.org), or on-line hypertext (http://www.fee.org/pdf/books/The_Law.pdf, or http://www.constitution.org/law/bastiat.htm)

I, Pencil, Leonard Read, The Freeman, FEE, the Foundation for Economic Education (http://www.fee.org/pdf/books/I,%20Pencil%202006.pdf)

Foundations of Morality, Henry Hazlitt, 1964 (http://www.fee.org/pdf/the-freeman/yeager1104.pdf)

The Protestant Ethic and the Spirit of Capitalism, Max Weber, trans. T. Parsons, Dover Publications, 2003-ed. NY (http://xroads.virginia.edu/~HYPER/WEBER/cover.html)

Declaration of Independence and the Constitution of the United States, see Heritage Foundations TownHall.com site or go to (http://www.constitution.org/usdeclar.pdf, http://www.usconstitution.net/const.pdf)

The Moral Foundations of Society, paper by: Margaret Thatcher, Center for Constructive Alternatives Seminar, concluding lecture, Hillsdale College, Nov, 94 (http://www.hillsdale.edu/news/imprimis/archive/issue.asp?year=1995&month=03)

Property & the Moral Life, article by: Jason Baldwin, The Freeman: Ideas on Liberty, Feb, 98, FEE (http://www.thefreemanonline.org/featured/property-and-the-moral-life/)

Common Sense, paper by American Founding Father: Thomas Paine, 1776 (http://odur.let.rug.nl/~usa/D/1776-1800/paine/CM/sensexx.htm)

Entrepreneurship, Religion and Business Ethics, research paper with results on survey of 10,000 'business professionals', Longenecker, McKinney & Moore, Baylor University (http://www.usasbe.org/knowledge/proceedings/1998/16-Longenecker.PDF)

C. Quotations through the Ages :

George Washington:

"It is substantially true that virtue or morality is a necessary spring of popular government. The rule, indeed, extends with more or less force to every species of free government." (1796, Farewell Speech).

John Adams:

"Our Constitution was designed only for a moral and religious people. It is wholly inadequate for the government of any other." (2nd president of the United States, 1789)

Thomas Paine:

"The cause of America is in a great measure the cause of all mankind."

"A long habit of not thinking a thing wrong, gives it a superficial appearance of being right."

"Society in every state is a blessing, but government even in its best state is but a necessary evil in its worst state an in tolerable one; for when we suffer, or are exposed to the same miseries by a government, which we might expect in a country without government, our calamities is heightened by reflecting that we furnish the means by which we suffer!"

(Common Sense, Philadelphia, Feb. 14, 1776)

Winston Churchill:

"It has been said that democracy is the worst form of government except all the others that have been tried."

Ronald Reagan:

"More than 200 years after the patriots fired that first shot heard 'round the world, one revolutionary idea still burns in the hearts of men and women everywhere: A society where man is not beholden to government; government is beholden to man." (March 2, 1984).

Margaret Thatcher:

"Free societies demand more care and devotion than any others. They are, moreover, the only societies with moral foundations, and those foundations are evident in their political, economic, legal, cultural, and, most importantly, spiritual life."

"I am an enthusiast of democracy because it is about more than the will of the majority. If it were only about the will of the majority, it would be the right of the majority to oppress the minority. The American Declaration of Independence and Constitution make it clear that this is not the case. There are certain rights which are human rights and which no government can displace."

"It was two members of the intellectual elite, Marx and Lenin, who conceived of "dialectical materialism," the basic doctrine of communism. It robs people of all freedom - from freedom of worship to freedom of ownership. Marx and Lenin desired to substitute their will not only for all individual will but for God's will. They wanted to plan everything; in short, they wanted to become gods. Theirs was a breathtakingly arrogant creed, and it denied above all else the sanctity of human life."

"If no individual can be trusted with power indefinitely, it is even more true that no government can be. It has to be checked, and the best way of doing so is through the will of the majority, bearing in mind that this will can never be a substitute for individual human rights."

"Tyrants are not moved by idealism. They are moved by naked ambition. Idealism did not stop Hitler; it did not stop Stalin."

Lord Acton:

"Power tends to corrupt, and absolute power corrupts absolutely."

Benjamin Franklin: Arguably America's first Entrepreneur. Inventor of the bifocals, modern insurance, the Post Office, urinary catheter, lightning rod, Franklin stove, odometer, University of Pennsylvania, and Poor Richard's Almanac.

"Wealth is not his that has it but his that enjoys it."
"Where liberty reigns, there is my country."

"God grant that not only the love of liberty but a thorough knowledge of the rights of man may pervade all the nations of the earth, so that a philosopher may set foot anywhere on its surface and say: 'This is my country.' "

"If you can't pay for a thing, don't buy it. If you can't get paid for it, don't sell it. Do this and you will have calm and drowsy nights, with all of the good business you have now and none of the bad."

Confucius: (551BC - 479BC, Chinese philosopher, The Analects}

"To see what is right and not to do it is want of courage."

Henry Ford: (1863 – 1947, American industrialist)

"A business that makes nothing but money is a poor kind of business."

Robert Noyce: (inventor of the silicon chip)

"If ethics are poor at the top, that behavior is copied down through the organization."

John D. Rockefeller, Jr.: (1839-1937, American entrepreneur)

"I believe that every right implies a responsibility; every opportunity an obligation; every possession a duty."

Marvin Bower: (former managing partner of McKinsey & Company)

"There is no such thing as business ethics. There is only one kind - you have to adhere to the highest standards."

Isaac Asimov: (1920 - 1992, Russian writer and scientist)

"Never let your sense of morals prevent you from doing what is right."

Albert Einstein: (1879-1955; German-born American theoretical physicist)

"Relativity applies to physics, not ethics."

D. The 13 Virtues of Benjamin Franklin:

These are the 13 key virtues that Benjamin Franklin believed were necessary to be an Entrepreneur and a just man. They were, in his opinion, the fundamental principles that each American must follow to live the promise and potential of the original 13 "United States" of America. They apply equally to the citizen of today's greatly-expanded 50-state Union.

1 Temperance	8 Justice
2 Silence	9 Moderation
3 Order	10 Cleanliness
4 Resolution	11 Tranquility
5 Frugality	12 Chastity
6 Industry	13 Humility
7 Sincerity	

www.ingramcontent.com/pod-product-compliance
Lightning Source LLC
Chambersburg PA
CBHW030614290326
41930CB00049B/352